Writing and Editing Checklists

Everything You Need to Take Your Book from First Draft to Publication

K.M. Allan

Copyright © 2025 by K.M. Allan

All rights reserved.

No portion of this book may be reproduced in any form without written permission from the publisher or author.

NO AI TRAINING: Without in any way limiting the author's [and publisher's] exclusive rights under copyright, any use of this publication to "train" generative artificial intelligence (AI) technologies to generate text is expressly prohibited. The author reserves all rights to license uses of this work for generative AI training and development of machine learning language models.

First Edition.

Paperback ISBN: 978-0-6487730-8-5

Ebook ISBN: 978-0-6487730-9-2

Contents

Just Start   1

How to Use This Book   2

Writing Elements   7

1. The Show Don't Tell Checklist   8
2. The Deep POV Checklist   16
3. The Five Senses Checklist   23
4. The Tension Checklist   28
5. The Backstory Checklist   37
6. The Payoff Checklist   44
7. The Action Beats Checklist   49
8. The Settings Checklist   54
9. The POV Checklist   61
10. The Foreshadowing Checklist   69
11. The Plot Twist Checklist   76
12. The Info-Dumping Checklist   81
13. The Conflict Checklist   86
14. The Unpredictability Checklist   91
15. The Head Hopping Checklist   95

16. The Assumptions Checklist	100
17. The Coincidences Checklist	105
18. The World-Building Checklist	110
19. The Internal Thoughts Checklist	118
20. The Stakes Checklist	125
21. The Dialogue Tips Checklist	129
Outlining	**137**
22. The Reverse Outline Checklist	138
Drafts	**142**
23. The Three Draft Checklist	143
24. The Final Draft Checklist	147
Word Count	**154**
25. The Reduce a Big Word Count Checklist	155
26. The Under Writing Checklist	160
27. The Over Writing Checklist	166
Openings	**171**
28. The Book Openings Checklist	172
Endings	**178**
29. The Chapter Endings Checklist	179
30. The Book Endings Checklist	184
Characters	**192**
31. The Distinct Characters Checklist	193
32. The Character Motivation Checklist	201
33. The Describing Without a Mirror Checklist	205

Scenes	210
34. The What to Establish in a Scene Checklist	211
35. The Scene Sequel Checklist	216
36. The Action Scene Checklist	222
37. The Scene Isn't Working Checklist	231
The Art of Editing	238
38. The Early Draft Cuts Checklist	239
39. The Author Blind Spot Checklist	245
40. The Review Draft Checklist	250
41. The Edit Letter Checklist	256
Rewrites	263
42. The Something Is Missing Checklist	264
43. The Bare Minimum Checklist	272
Proofing	278
44. The Proofreading Checklist	279
45. The Fresh Eyes Typo Hunting Checklist	283
Editing Elements	288
46. The Delete Checklist	289
47. The Weak Word Checklist	292
48. The Active Checklist	295
49. The Stage Direction Checklist	298
50. The Dialogue Checklist	303
51. The Chapter Checklist	308
52. The Little Details Checklist	315

53. The Repeats Checklist	322
Afterword	327
Thank You!	328
Acknowledgements	329
About the Author	330
Also by K.M. Allan	331

Just Start

When I launched my blog in 2017, the first post was titled *Just Start*. It was (as you can probably guess) about starting something you previously feared to do and included the still relatable quote:

"Start now. Start where you are. Start with fear. Start with pain. Start with doubt... just start." —Ijeoma Umebinyuo

Just start became a personal motto after that. It's something I do to write a book, put myself out there, or to create a blog post. And it was something I did after deciding to sort through 7 years' worth of blog content and rewrite the most helpful ones into checklists to create my first non-fiction book.

This idea was also sparked by the encouragement of wonderful writing friends, and the readers of my blog who let me know how helpful the original posts have been to them.

While these checklists can't cover every single aspect of writing and editing, I hope that what's here will help you create a base sturdy enough to pen your books—no matter if it's your first or your fiftieth.

The information here helped me improve all of my drafts, and if you've bought this book, you're doing the same for your own writing.

I wish you the very best of luck with it. All you have to do is *just start*.

— K.M. Allan

How to Use This Book

Just as every writer has their own process, this book is designed to be used in a way that will work for *you*.

Reading it from start to finish will provide you with all the tips and advice needed for writing and editing, but you can also jump to the checklists that interest you, and revisit them as you're writing and editing to make them part of your process.

All of these checklists were written from personal experience, and I have tried to keep the similar info overlap to a minimum. What works works, though, and you'll find that the same tips and topics do pop up on different checklists. Some contain examples from two of my four books, *Blackbirch: The Beginning* and *Blackbirch: The Dark Half*, or use my long-running blog example characters, Carla, and Jenny.

As I want you to use these checklists *your way*, I'm not going to provide a rigid guide, but if you'd like suggestions, this is how I use the checklists.

Checklist Example

To start, I'll go through...

- **The Three Draft Checklist**

After a first draft has been completed (and at various times throughout the writing/editing process) I'll use...

- **The Reverse Outlining Checklist**

Once the *Reverse Outline* has allowed me to get the story straight in my head and on paper, I'll use any checklist in the *Writing Elements* section that'll get my draft to the next stage.

- **The Show Don't Tell Checklist**
- **The Deep POV Checklist**
- **The Five Senses Checklist**
- **The Tension Checklist**
- **The Backstory Checklist**
- **The Payoff Checklist**
- **The Action Beats Checklist**
- **The Settings Checklist**
- **The POV Checklist**
- **The Foreshadowing Checklist**
- **The Plot Twist Checklist**
- **The Info-Dumping Checklist**
- **The Conflict Checklist**
- **The Unpredictability Checklist**
- **The Head Hopping Checklist**
- **The Assumptions Checklist**
- **The Coincidences Checklist**
- **The World-Building Checklist**
- **The Internal Thoughts Checklist**

- The Stakes Checklist
- The Dialogue Tips Checklist

When it feels like my writing elements are nailed, I'll spend a few drafts making sure the other elements of my books are on point, such as my characters and scenes, using any combination of the following checklists...

- The Distinct Characters Checklist
- The Character Motivation Checklist
- The Describing Without a Mirror Checklist
- The What to Establish in a Scene Checklist
- The Scene Sequel Checklist
- The Action Scene Checklist
- The Scene Isn't Working Checklist

Then I'll go over...

- The Book Openings Checklist
- The Chapter Endings Checklist
- The Book Endings Checklist

At this stage, if my word count is too big or too small, I'll run through the right checklist for the situation...

- The Reduce a Big Word Count Checklist
- The Under Writing Checklist
- The Over Writing Checklist

After editing down or upping my word count, I usually have a manuscript that is as solid as I can make it, so I'll move onto editing and run through the checklists that suit my purposes in the *Editing Elements* section.

- **The Early Draft Cuts Checklist**
- **The Author Blind Spot Checklist**
- **The Review Draft Checklist**
- **The Something Is Missing Checklist**
- **The Bare Minimum Checklist**

It's usually now that I'll send my MS to beta readers, if I haven't already. Depending on what they say, I may go back through some of the checklists. I'll then write myself an edit letter.

- **The Edit Letter Checklist**

Although beta feedback is always helpful, it's also a lot to take in, especially if an overwhelming amount of changes are required or you've been given conflicting opinions/advice. That can shake confidence in a manuscript, and an edit letter can help you gain some of it back.

After that, I'll do a final check using the proofing checklists.

- **The Proofreading Checklist**
- **The Fresh Eyes Typo Hunting Checklist**

Once the overall story is set in place, I'll move to the *Editing Elements* section. I keep these specific checklists until last because they take time and are tedious, but they also signal that the end is in sight!

- **The Delete Checklist**
- **The Weak Word Checklist**
- **The Active Checklist**
- **The Stage Direction Checklist**
- **The Dialogue Checklist**
- **The Chapter Checklist**

- **The Little Details Checklist**

- **The Repeats Checklist**

For my last checklist, I'll complete the items I *haven't* done yet on the...

- **The Final Draft Checklist**

Now, before *you* get overwhelmed, please keep in mind that I *don't* use every single checklist when working on a manuscript, and I don't run through every single item—and you don't have to either.

What I *do* use is what works for me to shape my book into the best version I can make it. That's the purpose of *this* book, and I hope it helps you to do the same.

Writing Elements

The following checklists delve into the writing elements that can level up your sentences. Here, you'll learn how to show instead of tell, use deep point of view to create a connection between the readers and your characters, use foreshadowing, conflict, and internal thoughts correctly, learn how to avoid info-dumping, and head hopping, make the most of your dialogue, and many other writing tips and tricks.

The Show Don't Tell Checklist

SHOW, DON'T TELL. It's one of the most spouted pieces of writing advice, and one of the most confusing.

When I first heard of it, I had no idea what it meant. Surely writing that my character *"rose from her chair and walked across the room"* was showing? Yes? No? Maybe?

No. It's a no. A hard no. It's "telling" the reader what the character is doing (and in a very uninspired way).

Showing is using your words to create a picture in the reader's mind, to allow them to feel as if they are the characters. That it's them *"pulling their tired bones from the stiff seat and shuffling across the dusty floorboards."*

It's all about forging a connection between the reader and the characters, and as this checklist will prove, it isn't as confusing as you think.

Find and Replace the Telling Words

We all have words we repeat or unnecessary words we delete to strengthen our prose. Other words we should pay attention to as we edit (for the millionth time) are "telling" words. These are words or phrases that make our sentences read as if we are telling what is happening instead of using words that show or invoke images.

The way to track down these tells is using your *find/search* tool and reevaluating any sentence containing the telling words found on the checklist at the end of these tips.

Examples: *(Taken from Blackbirch: The Beginning)*

Telling: When she returned with lunch, Max had demolished most of his meal. Even so, **he looked hungrily** at the chicken sandwich Sarah handed to Josh.

Showing: When she returned with lunch, Max had demolished most of his meal. Even so, **he licked his lips** at the chicken sandwich Sarah handed to Josh.

Such a small, simple change, but removing the "looked hungrily" and replacing it with "licked his lips" not only implies "hunger" but makes for a more interesting, visual read.

Telling phrases such as "began to" or "started to" can almost always be swapped for something active, instantly taking your words from tell to show.

Delve Into Deep POV

Along with showing and not telling, adding Deep POV to your arsenal of writers' tricks will lift your game.

Deep POV is essentially writing the story from the character's POV—everything they see, think, and feel—and goes very much hand-in-hand with show, don't tell.

Examples: *(Taken from Blackbirch: The Beginning)*

Telling: The pain traveled **down Josh's head**, across his neck and into his shoulders where it pooled on his left side, waking it from its numb state. **The sensation was surprising at first**, then it was replaced with sharpness. It was not a pain caused by power or flames, but one borne from metal and unforgiving edges.

Showing: The pain traveled **down his cheek**, across his neck and into his shoulders where it pooled on the left, waking the inner muscles from their numb state. **Josh's mouth dropped open at the sensation before his lips drew back and**

he grimaced at the sharpness. It was not a suffering caused by power or fire, but one borne from metal and unforgiving edges.

Did you feel the pain in the showing example? Was it a better read than the telling sensation which stated Josh's surprise at the sharpness rather than showing how it affected his body? That's the magic of Deep POV—and a great companion of show, don't tell.

Avoid Naming Emotions

An easy tell to spot and correct is emotions. Think sentences that say "she yelled angrily" or "he looked sad." Any part of your manuscript that names an emotion rather than representing it through dialogue, character action, or physical reactions should be given a second look and rewritten when possible.

Examples: *(Taken from Blackbirch: The Beginning)*

Telling Emotion: ...having to spend it with Sarah and listening to her mock Eve's beliefs. It **angered** Eve, especially when those ideals were something they had both once shared. Now Sarah treated her the way everyone else did.

Showing Emotion: ...having to spend it with Sarah and listening to her mock Eve's beliefs. **She squeezed her closed fists at the memory, concentrating on the sharp pinch of fingernails in her skin.** Those ideals were something they once shared. Now Sarah treated her the same way everyone else did.

De-Tag and Make the Most of Your Dialogue

A great way to slot in showing without endless paragraphs of description is to look at where you can de-tag your dialogue of the common "he said," "she explained," and throw in action beats.

Examples: *(Taken from Blackbirch: The Beginning)*

Telling Tag: "When everyone thinks you're doing what they expect, they get comfortable," **Eve explained her attire.** "When they stop noticing you, you're free to do the unexpected."

Showing Action Beat: "When everyone thinks you're doing what they expect, they get comfortable." **Eve swept her hand through her hair and then smoothed her open palm along her polo shirt and jeans.** "When they stop noticing you, you're free to do the unexpected."

Using dialogue is also a great way to add in show instead of telling what the character said or did.

Examples: *(Taken from Blackbirch: The Beginning)*

Telling: Dr. Chen appeared in the doorway next to ask Josh to follow her upstairs for his final tests. **She wanted him to change into a hospital gown but he refused, allowing the bad mood Arden put him in to color his curt response.**

Showing With Dialogue: Dr. Chen appeared in the doorway next, her petite frame barely filling it. **"Are you ready to head upstairs?"**
"More tests?" Surely he'd done them all by now?
"The final tests. Do you want to slip into a gown, please?"
"No." Josh refused, allowing the bad mood Arden put him in to color his curt response.

Watch Your Staging

This goes back to our character rising out of their chair example at the start of this checklist.

While showing will give a sense of place and setting, what you don't need to do is stage direct. How a character got from point A to point B is (in most cases) irrelevant unless it's critical to the plot.

Examples: *(Taken from Blackbirch: The Beginning)*

Staging: Sarah could see his car parked out the front of the store. Her mom's van was parked around the back and was easier to get to by going through the rear courtyard. They began gathering their things together to head that way. Max gave her a goofy smile as she went to lock the door behind him.

Need To Know: Her mom had parked out the back, so Sarah followed Max to the front door to lock it behind him. "Race you home," he dared her, throwing Sarah a goofy smile as she pushed the door shut.

Not only does letting go of the staging cut down on unnecessary words, but it increases the pacing. This will keep your readers turning the page instead of putting down the book because you drowned them in descriptions of how a character got out of bed or moved from their house to the car.

Get Active

Active, present tense—whatever you want to call it—writing in a way that shows what your character is doing rather than telling what they did, ticks the "Show, don't tell" box and ramps up your action, pacing, and tension.

Examples: *(Taken from Blackbirch: The Beginning)*

Telling: He jumped out of bed, his exit far from graceful thanks to the bedsheet wrapped around his ankles, and found himself amongst a scattering of books, photo frames, and mailing bags.

Showing: Jumping out of bed, his feet caught, the bedsheet twisting itself tighter around his ankles. Falling to the floor in a messy heap, he groaned as his chest took the brunt of the hard wooden floor, and found himself amongst a scattering of books, photo frames, and mailing bags.

Using the active *"Jumping out of bed"* allows for the superior *"his feet caught, the bedsheet twisting itself tighter around his ankles"* showing instead of the telling *"his exit far from graceful thanks to the bedsheet wrapped around his ankles."*

It and adding in the more physical *"Falling to the floor in a messy heap, he groaned as his chest took the brunt of the hard wooden floor"* takes this paragraph to a show of the character falling out of bed, instead of just telling the reader it happened.

Get the Balance Right

As with most writing rules, just because you know the magic show, don't tell can add to your words, it doesn't mean you should use it *all the time*.

A book written completely from a showing perspective will overwhelm the reader and exhaust the writer. Not every sentence needs to be expanded into paragraphs of character movements, thoughts, feelings, and descriptions of detailed settings.

Sometimes telling works better and is preferable, for example, in an action scene where your sentences should be short and snappy. Stopping to show everything ruins the tension, so keep an eye on your show/tell balance.

Related Checklists

The Stage Direction Checklist
The Active Checklist
The Dialogue Checklist
The Deep POV Checklist

 The Show Don't Tell Checklist

○ **Find and Replace the Telling Words**
Use your *find/search* tool on the telling words listed in the second part of this checklist.

○ **Delve Into Deep POV**
Write the story from the character's POV—everything they see, think, and feel.

○ **Don't Name Emotions**
Give a second look at any part of your manuscript that names an emotion rather than representing it through dialogue, character action, or physical reactions.

○ **De-Tag and Make the Most of Your Dialogue**
Look where you can de-tag your dialogue of the common "he said" and throw in action beats.

○ **Watch Your Staging**
How a character got from point A to point B is (in most cases) irrelevant unless it's critical to the plot.

○ **Get Active**
Write in a way that shows what your character is doing rather than telling what they did.

○ **Get the Balance Right**
Not every sentence needs to be expanded into paragraphs of character movements, thoughts, feelings, and descriptions of detailed settings. Sometimes telling works better and is preferable.

The Show Don't Tell Checklist

FIND AND REPLACE THE TELLING WORDS

Use your *find/search* tool on these words and reevaluate any sentence containing them

- ○ Began to / Started to
- ○ Consider / Considered
- ○ Could see / Could hear / Could feel / Could smell
- ○ Decide / Decided
- ○ Feel / Felt
- ○ Hear / Heard
- ○ Hope / Hoped
- ○ Knew / Know
- ○ Look / Looked
- ○ Notice / Noticed
- ○ Realize / Realized / Realise / Realised
- ○ See / Saw
- ○ Seem / Seemed
- ○ Thought
- ○ Was
- ○ Watch / Watched
- ○ Were
- ○ When
- ○ Which
- ○ Wonder / Wondered

The Deep POV Checklist

IF YOU'VE NEVER HEARD of Deep Point of View, you're not alone. Or, if like me, you've heard about it and brushed it off because you write in third person omnipresent and don't need to worry about other POVs, this checklist should change your mind.

Deep POV is writing in a way that eliminates distance between the reader and your characters. It overlaps with the good old *Show, Don't Tell* rule and helps forge a character connection with your readers. A connection that will hopefully see them follow your characters across chapters and series.

Watch Your Filter Words

The best way to tackle Deep POV is to watch your filter worlds. These are the words most likely to create distance.

This suggestion isn't a call to delete these words completely, because they have a place, but if you can *watch* your use, you'll strengthen your writing and delve into the Deep POV that you want your characters to have.

For a full list of filter words, see the checklist at the end of these tips.

Examples: *(Taken from Blackbirch: The Beginning)*

Without Deep POV: Josh **saw** Grace in that area, it wasn't hard to miss her. She was simply an older version of Sarah, in the same tall, lean frame and with the same long, straight blond hair.

With Deep POV: Grace was in that area and was hard to miss. She was an older version of Sarah, with the same tall, lean frame and long, straight blond hair.

Using the filter word *"saw"* sets the sentence up to be "told" to the reader through the eyes of *the narrator*. When you remove it and rewrite the same scene from the eyes of *the character*, there's automatically a sense of "voice." The description of Grace also feels as if it comes from Josh's *opinion of her* rather than the "narrator" *describing her*.

Write from the Character's Perspective, Not the Narrator's

As we touched on above, writing your story from the character's perspective as much as possible is what Deep POV is all about. When you reduce the narrator (yes, even when writing in third person omnipresent) you create a three-dimensional character and get the reader invested. They will care about what is happening to your characters because they'll feel everything right along with them.

Examples: *(Taken from Blackbirch: The Beginning)*

Narrator: The dark clouds swelled with torrents of water and obstructed Eve's limited view further.

Character: Dark clouds swelled with torrents of water, obstructing Eve's view.

It's just another simple change, yet now the same sentence reads if it's happening/coming from the character rather than a distant narrator. Going for Deep POV also cuts down on the unnecessary words in the original sentence.

Don't tell the reader your main character has just seen the love of his life; write about the way his heartbeat quickens, his palms go clammy, and how he stutters when he says "Hello."

If the reader isn't experiencing your story's events through your character's eyes as much as possible, make sure they do.

Use Internal Thoughts/Dialogue/Observations

Internal thoughts and dialogue allow the reader to know the character on a personal level, and you'll need to know your characters intimately to pull it off.

It's all about writing what *the character sees/feels/thinks* when they walk into a room, *not* just a mechanical list of what's in the room.

Examples: *(Taken from Blackbirch: The Beginning)*

Without Internal Thoughts: Out in the hallway, Josh found blue-gray walls and little else. Even the nurses' station across from his room was empty.

With Internal Thoughts: Out in the hallway, he found institutional blue-gray walls and little else. ***Why was it so silent?*** His gooseflesh returned, but not because of the cold. He rubbed his arms. ***Was something watching him?*** He must be paranoid. There was no one around. Even the nurses' station was empty.

As for a character's observations for themselves, instead of writing *"Her cheeks flushed pink"* try *"The heat rose through her cheeks"* to take readers inside the character's POV/body.

Stick to the Character's Knowledge

The quickest way to take yourself out of Deep POV is throwing in a sentence containing knowledge the POV character *doesn't* know. Stick to what they feel/see/can learn for themselves.

Comb through each chapter and look at the events your character has gone through and make sure you haven't accidentally given them knowledge they shouldn't have. It's easy to do when you're the author and know every plot point inside out, but be thorough. Work out who knows what, and make sure it all matches up to keep your deep POV intact.

Use Fewer Dialogue Tags and More Actions Beats

Some writers like to use no dialogue tags at all, while others stick to "said." Some vary by using "gasped" etc. Whatever your dialogue preferences, when it comes to Deep POV, less is more.

If you want to go full Deep POV, try to only use dialogue tags for clarity or when there are multiple characters in a scene, and swap them out for action beats/internal voice instead.

Example: *(Taken from Blackbirch: The Beginning)*

"Are you okay?" **The white T-shirt the girl had on was stained too. Black ash spoiled her appearance.**
She shifted her dark eyes to his face. "I could ask you the same thing." **She tilted her chin at his shirt.**
"It's not my blood."
The girl's gaze drifted back to his shoulder. "Are you sure?"
He wasn't. "I'm sick."
"You're not sick."
"I'm not?" **Why was he here then? In that bed, in that room? What kind of hospital was this?**

Write in an Active Voice

An all-around great writing tip, and something you should aim for anyway, is writing in an active voice.

For Deep POV, an active voice puts the reader right into the action. And when you combine that with what the characters' feel and think, you've not only mastered Deep POV but should also find you've got an awesome book on your hands.

Check Your Info-Dumps

If you want the reader to know how a world works, how characters know each other, the layout of the room they're in, it's easy to just dump it in a paragraph or write the setting likes it's a guided tour—i.e. *"The right side of the room was filled with bookshelves, the left half, a couch, and a brown coffee table with a lamp."*

Instead, check that you've worked those details into your story through the deep POV of your characters.

Is the main character staring at a generic list of furniture (couch, coffee table, armchair), searching for their car keys? Or are they pawing through crumb-filled couch cushions, coating the tips of their fingers in who knows what on the hunt for the missing keys?

Go deeper with the info you're delivering to the reader and make sure you're giving it to them from a personal, physical perspective (where it suits the story) instead of just info-dumping. That way, you know you're well and truly in the spotlight of Deep POV.

Related Checklists

The Show Don't Tell Checklist
The Internal Thoughts Checklist
The Info-Dumping Checklist
The Active Checklist
The Action Beats Checklist
The Dialogue Tips Checklist
The POV Checklist

 The Deep POV Checklist

☐ **Write from the Character's Perspective**
If the reader is not experiencing story events through your character's eyes as much as possible, make sure they do.

☐ **Use Internal Thoughts/Dialogue/Observations**
Use internal thoughts, dialogue, and character observations to help the reader know the character on a personal level.

☐ **Stick to the Character's Knowledge**
Write what the characters can feel/see/learn for themselves and make sure you haven't given them knowledge they shouldn't have/know.

☐ **Use Fewer Dialogue Tags and More Actions Beats**
Use dialogue tags for clarity or only when there are multiple characters in a scene, and swap them for action beats/internal voice where suitable.

☐ **Write in an Active Voice**
Remember that active voice puts the reader right into the action.

☐ **Check Your Info-Dumps**
Work details in through the character's POV instead of info-dumping generic furniture/setting/backstory descriptions.

✓ The Deep POV Checklist

WATCH YOUR FILTER WORDS

Use your **find/search** tool on these words.
Don't delete all instances, but limit them where you can.

- ○ Decide / Decided
- ○ Feel / Felt
- ○ Hear / Heard
- ○ Knew / Know
- ○ Look / Looked
- ○ Notice / Noticed
- ○ Realize / Realise / Realized / Realised
- ○ See / Saw
- ○ Though
- ○ Watch / Watched
- ○ Wonder / Wondered

The Five Senses Checklist

When it comes to writing, the deeper the connection with the reader, the better your book will be, and one such way to do this is by using the five senses.

This involves using sight, sound, smell, touch, and taste in your descriptions and character actions. You can, of course, also include *The Sixth Sense* if your story involves seeing dead people or Bruce Willis.

Sight

Sight is obviously the easiest to add because characters do a lot of looking, watching, and describing what they see in the world around them.

How you invoke sight on a sense level is to go deeper, using emotion, color, and texture to really give life to what your characters see.

> **Example:** *(Taken from Blackbirch: The Beginning)*
>
> He followed her gaze. The darkness deepened and spread, the black tainting the green surrounding it and changing the beauty of the trees. Deep, jagged cracks opened along the smooth bark as it melted and twisted into rough chunks. The shape of the trunks deformed. Leaves blackened and curled at the edges while the branches wilted under their weight.

Black tainted green. Deep, jagged cracks. Smooth bark melting and twisting. Leaves blackening and curling. Branches wilting.

These are descriptive words that invoke the image of rotted trees in a way that's more visceral than just simply writing *"He followed her gaze and saw dark, rotted trees,"* don't you think?

Sound

Sound is one of those tricky senses. It comes off perfectly in a visual medium like TV because a viewer can hear (or not hear) what eerie silence is like. In book form, writing "the room was eerily silent" doesn't have the same level of impact.

That doesn't mean you can't use sound to add something to extra to your scenes, you just need to get more creative with it. Instead of struggling to describe how something might sound, use your words to invoke realism, tension, or reactions to sound.

Take, for example, a traffic jam. If you're stuck in one you might hear engines hum, the muffled bass thump of loud music through rolled up windows, car horns honked in the distance by impatient drivers at the back of the queue. You can invoke these sounds using your words. You can also make the reader feel them.

Example: *(Taken from Blackbirch: The Beginning)*

> The siren split the air, the high pitch stinging Josh's eardrums after making his body flinch. Palms pressed to ears, he peered out the doorway in search of the source.

When using sounds, play with them. Footsteps echoing in the dark can add great mystery. A sound perceived as imagined or misunderstood by a character adds tension. Create a relaxed mood with trickling water, or action with a rush of crashing waves.

Smell

Ah, smell. A sense that can either be wonderful or woeful—the stark difference of fresh-baked cookies versus decaying flesh.

When adding the smell sense to your words, it's great to pair it with real-world comparisons and universal memories.

Example: *(Taken from Blackbirch: The Beginning)*

The wintergreen scent perfumed the air and the clean mint burned in his nostrils. It was as strong as the earthy grit of dirt that coated his throat that day, etching the aroma into his soul. Sometimes he dreamt of those smells, waking in the morning to find they'd clung to him as he slept.

Perfumed air. Clean mint. Aroma. All words that invoke a feeling of scent. Mixed with a real world comparison of *"the earthy grit of dirt"* and it's a sensory delight.

Smells are one sense where the written word has an advantage over visual media such as movies, so be sure to use it. Have a character lament about a lost love when they walk past a florist flush with fresh blooms. Or a mystery plotline kicked off by the discovery of a nausea-inducing scent wafting from a creepy basement.

Taste

Taste can be one of the easier senses to invoke. After all, food is a big part of both the real world and any fictional ones. It can be slotted into your writing through descriptions of how food looks and tastes, or used as an effective way to bring about nostalgia by linking it to favorite foods and childhood memories.

Example: *(Taken from Blackbirch: The Beginning)*

Sarah snapped a young twig off the black birch as she pushed through another patch of cluttered trunks, chewing on the end as they emerged in an open area. The minty sweetness coated her tongue, giving her mouth a burst of winter coolness, reminding her of her childhood before the reality of the night caused her stomach to drop.

Later in this same scene, this taste sense is brought up again and used to reflect the darker turn the story takes:

"What is this place?" Sarah's stomach turned. Saliva filled her mouth, but it tasted of acid, bitter and sharp, overtaking the sweet black birch sap.

By incorporating taste into your work, you can add more depth to scenes, especially if you also tie it to an emotion or a great simile.

Touch

If you want to enhance your story world, touch is the sense for you. Characters touching objects, walls, furniture etc, not only creates a sense of setting but also brings it alive.

It's the same deal if you want to bring about a connection between characters. A hug during a time of need brings comfort, or a vise-like grasp around someone's wrist builds drama and tension.

Touch isn't just limited to physically feeling objects or others, though. You can also impart the sense in different ways.

> **Example:** *(Taken from Blackbirch: The Beginning)*
>
> He licked his sandpaper tongue across his dry lips and swallowed.

Did you immediately picture dry lips or recall how it feels to have them? The universal truth of never having chap-stick on hand leads to a description anyone can relate to, all made possible by invoking the sense of touch.

As you can see, using sight, sound, smell, touch, and taste can really add something special to your words. How often you use the five senses in writing is up to you. If you can invoke the senses in every scene, go for it, but don't force it. Use them organically and combine them together to make your fictional world come alive.

Related Checklists

The World-Building Checklist
The Settings Checklist

The Five Senses Checklist

◯ **Sight**
Go deeper than a basic description and use emotion, color, and texture to give life to what your characters see.

◯ **Sound**
Instead of describing how something might sound, use your words to invoke realism, tension, or reactions to sound. Footsteps echoing in the dark can add great mystery.

◯ **Smell**
Pair smell descriptors with real-world comparisons and universal memories, such as a character lamenting about a lost love after walking past a florist and sniffing the fresh blooms.

◯ **Taste**
Slot taste into your writing through descriptions of how food looks and tastes, or bring about some nostalgia by linking it to favorite foods and childhood memories.

◯ **Touch**
Use characters touching objects, walls, and furniture to create a sense of setting and to also bring it alive. Same deal for character connections. A hug during a time of need brings comfort, or a vise-like grasp around someone's wrist builds drama.

The Tension Checklist

HAVE YOU EVER READ a book where you couldn't flip the page fast enough, resenting all of life's distractions until you could reach the final chapter?

While novels like this are no doubt filled with terrific or terrifying characters, real dialogue, and surprising plot twists, they also contain the one thing that makes your readers eager to see what happens next: *tension*.

Adding tension to your story is like putting frosting on a cake. The frosting is arguably the best part of the cake, and tension is like that too.

It draws the reader in; they want more, right until the last sentence, when all the delicious cake-story has been devoured. Create that now by using this checklist to bake tension right into your book.

Not So Easy-Peasy

In those rare moments in life when things are going pretty well and nothing dramatic is happening, everything is easy-peasy.

It's also *boring* and not the ideal model to base a book on. No reader wants to read chapter after chapter of your character going about their life, always winning. They need drama. Highs. Lows. Not easy. Not peasy. And that is where the tension comes in.

- Make things hard.
- Give your characters a win.
- Make it hard again.

Hitchhike Through Obstacle City

Okay, so maybe you don't want to make things *too* hard. That might not suit your genre and that's fine. But every genre can add tension by hitchhiking their characters through obstacle city.

They want to be with someone? Sure, they've got to fight for them first. They're about to land their dream job? Okay, but that last-minute snafu with their presentation will put it in doubt.

- Put a big obstacle in the way.
- Put a small obstacle in the way.
- Add something, or a series of somethings, to create tension.
- Pave the road forward with bumps.

Sure, you could write a book where nothing really bad happens and the characters all get what they want with little effort or fuss, but would anyone want to read it?

The answer is *no*. Readers want characters who get what they want *after* they've been through hell. You get that kind of tension by making events more complicated than they need to be.

Unless the plot or genre calls for it, we're not talking ridiculously complicated, but just complicated enough. For example, say that your character needs to go across town to pick up an item by a certain time. Normally, such a mundane event would go off without a hitch. But not in *your* story.

In your tension-packed tome, the main character's car won't start. Then they miss the bus. Then the Rideshare that arrives is driven by a pregnant lady who—you guessed it—goes into labor. A simple drive across town becomes a complicated event full of tension. And your readers will love it.

Get Yourself a One-Armed Man

If you've seen *The Fugitive*, you'll know that Dr. Richard Kimble isn't believed about a one-armed man who killed his wife. This leads to a wrongful conviction, an escape en route to jail, and being pursued by US Marshals. These things alone create tension.

Now, I'm not suggesting your book has to have these specific forms of tension, but it needs to have the main one—which is doubt.

He wasn't believed about the one-armed man, and it created terrific tension. Do the same by...

- Having doubt amongst your characters.
- Upping tension with the characters paranoia about each other and each other's motives.
- Having the characters dislike each other.
- Having characters fight.
- Having characters brimming with mistrust.

Resolution Revolution

Conflicts make for great tension. You know what kills conflicts? Resolving them.

Your book needs to have resolutions to be a satisfying read, *but* resolving those conflicts—at least the big ones—too soon undoes that.

- Don't resolve things too early.
- As you resolve some of your early conflicts, keep the tension ample by introducing new conflicts.

Did your main character just find his long-lost twin? *Great.* Now up the tension by revealing the twin can't be trusted (there's *always* an evil twin).

Piggyback each resolution resolve with a *new* conflict to keep your tension tight throughout the whole story.

Be a Loser

Some would argue there are no stakes or tension without loss, and I would be one of those people. Loss is universal, everyone feels it in their lives, and so should your characters.

- Have them lose *something*.
- It can be as big as the love of their life.
- It can be as small as the package they need to deliver for their courier job.

Either way, they will feel that loss and it will drive the story forward in all of its tension-filled glory!

Hang Off Those Cliffs

Another great tip for injecting tension into your book is to end each scene or chapter with a cliffhanger.

It doesn't need to be a huge *OMG-it-was-the-long-lost-sister* moment. It can be as simple as your main character receiving an unexpected text message, or just a line of dialogue that throws a spanner into the works.

Whatever your cliffhanger type moment, make sure it suits what's happening. Don't throw out a shock for shock's sake.

- The best cliffhangers are credible moments within the story.
- These moments can shock, but they can also devastate, be happy, sad, or unexpected.

Add Unanswered Questions

Have you ever read a book that's just been okay? The premise is fine, the characters relatable enough, you aren't racing to pick it up every day, but you're not ready to boot it from your reading pile just yet. Then it happens. You come across *one* sentence that forms a question.

It could be the main character musing about her first love, an off-page character who doesn't seem like much until the info drops that they mysteriously disappeared. Now you're intrigued. Now you want to pick up that book and keep reading. The book has posed a question and now you want the answer.

- Unanswered questions build tension, and the best thing about them is that they can be big or small, and you don't have to limit yourself to just one.

- Your book can have an unanswered question in every chapter if you can plausibly swing it.

Just ensure that you answer the question at some point and kick off a new question to keep the tension going until the last page.

Put in Higher Stakes

Trying to get your main character across town to pick something up might be tension-filled when you throw complicated events into the mix, but if you want the tension to be even higher, you've got to raise the stakes.

What if the item your main character needs to pick up is life-saving medicine? What if it's a ransom needed to get their kidnapped child back?

- The higher the stakes, the tighter the tension, the more readers will want to keep reading.

Add a Ticking Clock

Imagine a character who has to be at the airport on Tuesday at noon to catch a flight he can't miss, and he gets there at the right time, the right day, and boards the plane. Not exactly thrilling, is it?

Now imagine that same character waking up late, or being involved in a car accident on the way to the airport. Perhaps the train they need to take is late, and then the bus, throwing their whole schedule off course and delivering a much more interesting read.

Suddenly, a specific appointment has an air of excitement to it, and a deadline readers will want to find out wasn't missed.

If your story is lacking some tension, and the plot allows for it...

- Give the main character a set date or time they need to be somewhere or to do something.
- Throw every (realistic) thing you can at them to stop them from getting to where they need to be.

Perfect Your Pacing

Of course, there's a place on the shelf for slow burn novels that reveal their genius at the very end with a twist the reader never saw coming, but you've got to convince readers to get to the last page first.

If you think your pacing could use some excitement...

- Mix up your chapter lengths.
- Jump into a succession of short, snappy scenes and barrel your readers through your story like a speeding train.
- Use short sentences during the most suspenseful passages.

These options will make for the perfect pacing in a tension-filled read. The genius twist at the end, though, is still up to you to create.

Drop a Mystery

Even if your story isn't a mystery, you can still add the elements—and some tension.

- Drop clues throughout your manuscript that seem unrelated but suddenly come together at the end to mix a little mystery into your plot.
- Ask various questions throughout the manuscript, adding new questions as each one gets answered.

This will keep the reader's tension level at an all-time high.

Reveal and Then Run

One of the biggest killers to a suspenseful read is not stopping the story once the excitement has reached its pinnacle.

Yes, have a proper ending that ties things up, but don't waste *all* the tension you built by dragging things out with ten more chapters or an epilogue that explains *every little thing*.

- Reveal your ending or the twist your suspense was leading to and then run.

If you've done your job, the reader will figure out what happened after without needing it spelled out in additional scenes—keeping your hard-earned tension intact.

Related Checklists

The Conflict Checklist
The Plot Twist Checklist
The Stakes Checklist
The Foreshadowing Checklist
The Coincidences Checklist
The Unpredictability Checklist

# The Tension Checklist

◯ **Avoid Easy-Peasy**
Make things hard. Give your characters a win. Make it hard again.

◯ **Use Obstacles**
Allow your characters to get what they want after you've made events more complicated than they need to be.

◯ **Add Doubt**
Invoke doubt amongst your characters so things are brimming with mistrust.

◯ **Resolve Resolutions and Then Add More**
Don't resolve things too early and keep the tension ample by introducing new conflicts when old ones are solved.

◯ **Invoke Loss**
Loss is universal, everyone feels it in their lives, and so should your characters, whether it's big or small.

◯ **Use Cliffhangers**
If your plot allows it, end each scene or chapter with a cliffhanger.

 The Tension Checklist

○ **Add Unanswered Questions**
Pose questions that readers will want answers to. Answer them, and kick off a new question.

○ **Put In Higher Stakes**
The higher the stakes, the tighter the tension, the more readers will want to keep reading.

○ **Add a Ticking Clock**
Give the main character a set date/time they need to be somewhere/do something and then try to stop them from achieving their goal.

○ **Perfect Your Pacing**
Use short scenes/sentences/chapters to build tension and a quick pace.

○ **Drop a Mystery**
Include clues and various questions throughout your manuscript to create an air of mystery.

○ **Reveal and Then Run**
Drop your reveal/twist and then end things. Don't drag everything on for ten more pages.

The Backstory Checklist

ONE KEY TO WRITING a book that connects with readers is including characters they care about.

Or hate. It can be characters they hate. Just as long as the readers want to follow from the first page to the last.

Follow-worthy characters have goals to achieve, obstacles to overcome, and a story worth following. An important layer to add to them, though, is the one that makes them *who* they are—and that's their backstory.

Don't Info-Dump

While you should avoid info-dumping any part of your book, info-dumping the backstory rates even higher. *Why?* Because it slows things down. This is especially true in the first three chapters of your book.

The beginning of the book is when you should hook the reader, not bore them with how the main character grew up in a small town, got high grades throughout school, moved to the city, found an apartment, then ended up the pawn in a serial killer's game. Start, and stay, with the game. At least for the first few chapters.

- The main character's history is better sprinkled throughout the book. If you dump the fact that they used to steal cars in the first chapter, it'll be long forgotten by the time a climax that requires those skills rolls around.

Plan or Perfect It

If you're an organized writer who works out your plot and writes character outlines before getting stuck in to a draft, crafting your backstory should be a cinch.

- Know where the story starts and ends.
- Have in-depth profiles of each character to help you.
- Make the most of your organized-self and plan your backstory as part of your outline too.

If you don't plan (waves to fellow pantsers), you won't know the backstory until *after* you've written the first draft. You can then perfect it on the next few (hundred) drafts, or reverse outline it and blend it in as if it was always part of your ~~evil plan~~ story.

Show the Effects First

Before revealing any backstory, get into the habit of showing the effects of your backstory.

A character who fears the dark, feels claustrophobic in crowds, can't sleep without the white noise of a TV, and carries a jumper with them in summer will read as someone with quirks. But when their backstory of being caught in a snowstorm and buried in their car in the silent, dark, cold is revealed, all of those quirks make perfect sense.

- Backstory forms your characters. Use it to your advantage.

Relevantly Right

If you want a backstory to earn its place, always make sure it's relevant to your character's actions.

Don't open the story with the main character swimming in the ocean if the backstory in chapter eight reveals watching *Jaws* as a child messed them up and they'd *never* swim in the ocean (which is totally a legit reason, right? I'm asking for a friend...).

Backstory should be relevant...

- To the plot—explaining events or being needed for the events to happen.
- For your character—explaining why they are the way they are, and/or their motivations.

Trigger It

While you could give your characters a backstory so devastating they can't think of anything but their past, it's more common (and realistic) that your backstory will be something that doesn't occupy their thoughts every waking second.

Instead, there will be things that trigger it.

- A smell could remind a parent of the cookies they baked with their kids every Sunday.
- The sight of a racing ambulance with blaring sirens could remind a driver of a car accident years before.

Trigger the backstory using the five senses for a natural read.

Don't Always Devastate

While a devastating backstory ups the tension, you can instill an interesting one without horror or loss.

Use a...

- Quirky mystery or good fortune to lead the characters to where they need to be instead of a devastating event.

Flashy Flashbacks

Some writers/readers love flashbacks, some loathe them. I'm a fan if they're done right.

- Keep the flashback short.

- Kick it off with a relevant trigger (avoid unnatural segue ways into a flashback).

- Use it to show *something*, such as motivation or answers to a question.

- The flashback should exist for a reason, not because you had a setting or description you wanted to use in your book.

If you're not a fan of flashbacks or devoting paragraphs to the backstory, it's also perfectly fine to work it into passing narrative instead. A past revealed in a line of dialogue or a one-sentence reference in a paragraph is sometimes all you need.

Play With the Delivery

While flashbacks or triggered memories are enough to venture into backstory territory, there are other ways, too.

Use...

- Letters.

- Texts.

- Emails.

- Voicemails.

- Recordings suddenly unearthed

- Diaries found in dusty boxes.

Get creative with it and play with the way you deliver your backstory.

Balance It Out

Unless your backstory is a device you're using, i.e. swapping between present day and the past every other chapter, keep the backstory to a minimum and balance it out.

- Don't feature backstory in all chapters/scenes.

After all, you've started the story where you have on purpose. Let the characters live in the present (or whatever timeline you've set) and only venture into their past for the reasons listed in this checklist.

Related Checklists

The Info-Dumping Checklist
The Foreshadowing Checklist
The Distinct Characters Checklist
The Assumptions Checklist
The Scene Sequel Checklist

✓ The Backstory Checklist

○ **Don't Info-Dump**
Sprinkle the main character's history throughout the book, not dumped in the first chapter to be forgotten by the time it's important.

○ **Plan or Perfect It**
Plan the backstory before writing, or reverse outline after writing, and blend it in like it was always part of the story.

○ **Show the Effects First**
Before revealing any backstory, show its effects on your character so that what a reader may dismiss as a quirk then makes perfect sense.

○ **Make It Relevant**
Backstory should be relevant to the plot (explaining events or needed for events to happen) or character (why they are the way they are, and/or their motivations).

○ **Trigger It**
For realism, don't make your backstory something occupying your character's every thought. Instead, trigger it when relevant using the five senses.

The Backstory Checklist

◯ **Don't Always Devastate**
You can instill an interesting backstory without horror or loss. Think quirky mystery or good fortune leading the characters to where they are.

◯ **Flashy Flashbacks**
Keep flashbacks short and make sure it exists for a reason.

◯ **Play With the Delivery**
Creatively deliver your backstory, using letters, texts, emails, voicemails, unearthed recordings, and found diaries.

◯ **Balance It Out**
Unless your backstory is a present day/past day device you're using, keep it to a minimum and balance it out.

The Payoff Checklist

IF YOU'VE READ A book where the ending or big dramatic twist is the culmination of all the clues, moments, or hints in the book, then you've encountered *The Payoff*.

The MC finally getting what they want. The villain losing (or winning). The end of a war. The start of a love story. The payoff could be any of these things and more.

It's the little plots tied up throughout, and it's closure for all that's gone before it. If that sounds like something you want to feature in your books (and why wouldn't you?) this is what to include in *your* payoff.

Build It

If you want to avoid a twist reveal coming out of nowhere (the worst), or leave readers feeling like the answer they waited 300 pages for was tacked on in the final chapter (even worse), you need build up.

- Use clues.
- Include foreshadowing.
- Drop hints along the way to build suspicion and tension.

This is the murderer being the unsettling neighbor introduced early on, the one who inserts themselves into the investigation and lies about his relationship with the victim (thanks, years of watching *Criminal Minds*).

His alibi looks solid then falls apart, his lies holding truth until they don't. He brings an *is it or isn't it?* cat-and-mouse game to the pages, raising and dashing your suspicions until the last nail-biting reveal.

It's a much better payoff than the murderer being the waiter barely mentioned in chapter six who served the victim coffee that *one* time.

There's no payoff in that. Build it up, pay it off.

Make It All Fire, No Smoke

Imagine using half your book to tease a villain as unbeatable, requiring the heroes to wage a war so epic there's no way there won't be serious, soul-crushing losses, and then have the final battle over within one page (or even worse, off page) with none of the maiming or devastation readers had been teased with since the opening paragraph.

It's just smoke when there's no fire, and your payoff requires the opposite of that. If you promise a battle to end all battles or foreshadow the loss of characters the reader cares about (not the random character introduced just to be killed off), follow through.

- Light the story on fire and watch it burn.

It Needs to Linger

The romance you've been building since the main characters crossed paths, that tension you weaved around them with every dialogue exchange and stolen glance not only needs a decent payoff, but one that lingers.

Readers don't want to wait half a book or series for two characters to *finally* get together, only to have that moment over and done in one sentence.

- Give readers time to process.
- Allow them the space to rejoice.
- Create the time to deal with the outcome of said payoff.

Let them linger in that moment and give it the detail and attention it deserves.

Don't Overuse It

For a payoff to work, it needs to be made up of little payoffs leading to a big payoff, just like in a detective story when small clues are gathered leading to the solve of the bigger mystery.

These payoffs shouldn't be overused, such as putting one in every single chapter, or the big ones repeated. If your payoff centers around the shocking death of a beloved character, imagine how disappointing (and predictable) it would be if you gave three other characters the same payoff fate. Now that first death, the one that could have been game-changing, is just the start of a tired storyline.

- Don't overuse or repeat your payoffs.
- Use them sparingly and harvest them for every ounce of emotional impact.

Keep It Subtle

The big payoff might be earth-shattering for your story or characters, but the little payoffs or the set-ups leading to it don't have to be. Sometimes, it's better that it's not.

For example, that necklace given to the main character as a birthday present was a touching moment in chapter three. By chapter twenty, we learn the ornate decorative pattern on the family heirloom is the key to unlocking an ancient language.

- Hide your set-ups in plain sight.
- Mix them up with other details that aren't little payoffs so the reader doesn't know what to expect. That doll found in a dusty box in the attic could be the clue to a mystery or just a doll.

Keep your set-ups subtle and the reader guessing which hint, event, or item given to your characters means something. It'll make the big payoff that much sweeter. Sweeter is what you want. Devastation is what you want. What you want is the *"Yes, I knew it!"* moments instead of the *"What? How/when/why did that even happen?"*

Master these checklist items and deliver *those* moments to your readers. It'll give your payoff the payoff it deserves.

Related Checklists

The Foreshadowing Checklist
The Tension Checklist
The Plot Twist Checklist
The Little Details Checklist

The Payoff Checklist

- ◯ **Build It**
  Use clues, foreshadowing, and hints to build into the payoff.

- ◯ **Make It All Fire, No Smoke**
  If you promise a battle to end all battles, follow through.

- ◯ **It Needs to Linger**
  Don't gloss over long-awaited moments.

- ◯ **Don't Overuse It**
  Use your payoffs sparingly and don't repeat them.

- ◯ **Keep It Subtle**
  Hide your payoff set-ups in plain sight to keep things unexpected.

The Action Beats Checklist

IF YOU'RE WONDERING WHAT an action beat is, it's an action your character is doing while they're talking.

Yeah, it's not exactly an earth-shattering revelation, is it? It's also something you've probably been doing naturally, but now that you know the name and meaning of this writing trick, it's time to put it to good use with this checklist.

Break up the Boring

When an action beat pairs with your dialogue, it breaks up the usual he said/she said monotony of dialogue tags.

Examples:

Dialogue Tag: "Hi," **Jenny said.**

Action Beat: "Hi." **Jenny lifted her hand, waving her fingers in Carla's face.**

Use your action beats to...

- Break up long passages of dialogue.
- Put pauses in the conversation.
- Give your pacing a boost.
- Add tension to a character conversation.
- Keep the reader on edge.

A character running from danger, fumbling with their keys at the door, is *always* more exciting than them just shouting for help with a boring "said" or "screamed" dialogue tag.

Examples:

Dialogue Tags:
"He's coming, hurry!" **Jenny said**.
"I'm trying," **Carla growled**.
"You're too late," **Jenny cried**. "We're dead! We're dead!"
"I've got it!" **Carla shouted**.

Action Beats:
"He's coming, hurry!" **Jenny latched onto Carla's arm**.
"I'm trying." **Carla shook Jenny's talon-like fingers off, fumbling for her keys**.
"You're too late." **Jenny sank against the door-frame**. "We're dead! We're dead!"
"I've got it!" **Carla felt the key click and turn, pushing on the door and shoving Jenny inside**.

Does that mean you should replace all dialogue tags with action beats? *No*. The key is to mix up the action beats, dialogue tags, and leave some dialogue untagged (when it's clear who's speaking) to give your dialogue the variety it needs to break up the boring.

Show and Don't Tell

If one of your writing goals is to get a handle on showing and not telling, action beats are a good way to ensure you're ticking that *show* box.

Examples:

Tell Dialogue Tag: "I had the worst day," **Carla said sadly**. "Everything went wrong."

Show Action Beat: "I had the worst day." **Carla's fingers trembled on the table before she lifted them to her cheek, wiping at the tears.** "Everything went wrong."

Does it add to your word count? *Yes*, but it paints a stronger picture of your character's emotional needs, puts some action into the sentence, and is more interesting to read.

Look for any dialogue tags you've capped off by outright stating the emotion (sad, angry, happy) and replace with an action beat that shows the reader the emotion instead.

Avoid Info-Dumping Setting

While there's nothing wrong with describing your setting in a well-written paragraph, there's a time and place in a story for such a thing. If stopping to info-dump the room your characters have walked into slows things down, consider using some well-placed action beats.

Examples:

Info-Dumped Setting:
Carla and Jenny stumbled into the house, throwing the door shut. There was a telephone sitting on the side table next to the couch on the far wall, lit by the yellow glow of the lamp beside the closed curtains.
"Call the police!" Carla shouted at Jenny. "He might still be out there."
"I hope he's gone," Jenny said. "Otherwise we're in trouble."
"Why?" Carla asked.
"There's no dial tone."

Action Beats Setting:
Carla and Jenny stumbled into the house, throwing the door shut.
"Call the police!" **Carla dragged Jenny to the couch and dared to part the closed curtains.** "He might still be out there."
"I hope he's gone." **Jenny's shaking fingers struggled with the telephone receiver.** "Otherwise we're in trouble."
"Why?" **Carla bumped against the side table, almost knocking down the**

lamp.
"There's no dial tone."

The reader still learns the setting of the house this way, so if it suits the scene and your dialogue, drop the setting descriptions into your action beats.

Sneak In Character Description

Just as action beats can portray your setting, they can also deliver the description of your characters. This gives you more options, meaning you don't have to resort to the old *look-in-a-mirror* cliché.

Example:

"What do you mean there's no dial tone?" **Carla brushed her dark bangs out of her eyes**.
"I don't know how else to say there's no dial tone, except there's no dial tone!" Jenny threw down the receiver.

While they can really add something extra to your sentences, remember that there's only so much action characters can do. Don't add a beat for the sake of it, and apply them like any other balanced writing trick to bring your story to life.

Related Checklists

The Dialogue Tips Checklist
The Info-Dumping Checklist
The Show Don't Tell Checklist
The Describing Without a Mirror Checklist

The Action Beats Checklist

◯ **Break up the Boring**
Replace the usual he said/she said monotony of dialogue tags, break up long passages of dialogue, add pauses to conversations, boost pacing, and add tension to conversations with action beats.

◯ **Show and Don't Tell**
Look for dialogue tags that state emotion and replace it with an action beat that shows the emotion instead.

◯ **Avoid Info-Dumping Setting**
If it suits the scene and your dialogue, drop the setting descriptions in your action beats.

◯ **Sneak In Character Description**
Avoid the old look-in-a-mirror cliché and use action beats to add the physical descriptions of your characters instead.

The Settings Checklist

When writing a book, plenty of effort goes into building our characters or working out our plots. Because of this, sometimes the setting of your book world gets lost.

This can happen if you're afraid of overwhelming the reader with too much detail, worried you'll slow the pace by stopping to explain things, or assuming they'll know everything because it's set in the modern world.

But skimping on your setting could deprive the reader of an immersive experience that adds a deeper layer to your story, so use this checklist to stop the settings from fading into the background.

Make It Authentic

Regardless of whether your book is set in a modern city, a '50s era small town, a futuristic otherworldly planet, or a hidden fantasy world filled with imaginative creatures, you can still make it authentic. You do this via specific details.

Examples:

Generic Details: They parked **the car** under the **large tree** and went into the **restaurant** for some **food**.

Specific Details: They parked **the Chevy** under the **large maple tree** and went into the **Cheese and Grill** for **warm, toasted cheese sandwiches**.

By adding specifics, it lifts the sentence to a more interesting, relatable place and gives the reader a vivid setting.

It's much easier to picture the truck pull up under the sprawling tree full of bright red leaves, and the warm, melty goodness of a grilled cheese sandwich than the very non-specific "car," "tree," and "food" in the first example. Details are key. Add them.

Weave It In

You don't need your characters to walk into a room and then describe the furniture around them to establish the setting, but you can't avoid describing it either. If you do, you'll risk the reader not getting a sense of where your characters are.

If the reason you haven't gone all out on your setting is that you don't want to info-dump or bore the reader, weave the description in instead.

Let the reader know the characters are in a kitchen because *"Carla threw her keys on the marble bench before flinging open the refrigerator door and grabbing a slice of leftover pizza."* It's better than a paint-by-numbers description, such as, *"Carla came into the kitchen looking for food, and passed the marble top island bench before reaching the tall refrigerator."*

Make It Balanced

As much as your setting can be another character or added layer to your book, it's *not* the main character.

Don't spam your readers with over-the-top detailed setting descriptions or go on for paragraphs at a time. If you find yourself getting bored or skipping the parts that delve into the setting too deeply, take that as a sign to pare it back.

On the flip side, if you're getting feedback from betas saying they don't understand the world or can't picture the places your characters live or visit, you might be too stingy with your setting details and need to add more.

It's a delicate balancing act, but one worth getting right.

Use Your Characters

A main character afraid of swimming in the ocean is going to only see the water as something dark and fearful and their take on their setting/world will reflect that. Another character at the same beach who has no fear of the water would see and interact with the setting much differently.

Use your character's perspectives, inner-truths, and history to your advantage when building a picture of your book's world, and let it color how the setting comes to life.

Don't Describe Everything at the Start

While it may seem logical to get the room settings out of the way and describe every inch of the surroundings as soon as your character enters them, this can drag things down.

Get into the habit of only mentioning what's necessary first, such as the door the main character walks through, or the couch they sit on. Then, as the scene plays out, have your character notice the other objects around them.

This way the room setting still gets described, but it doesn't happen all at once, or right at the start of the scene, potentially boring the reader or robbing your scene of tension and pacing.

Build a Picture

A known piece of writing advice for setting descriptions is no white rooms. If you haven't heard of the term before, this is when the writer has the character in a place but hasn't described it in enough detail, or at all. It happens. The characters end up floating around, carrying on in a scene that has no grounding because the writer has left out the room settings/surroundings.

It could be as simple as having a character sit on the edge of a bathtub and stare at themselves in the mirror above the vanity. You've only mentioned three things, but every reader will build the picture of a bathroom in their minds.

Avoid Sounding like a Salesperson

Hands up if you've read a book where the character walks into a room and every piece of furniture is described in such detail, you have to wonder if the writer's day job is working as a furniture salesperson. Sometimes it's possible to get *too* detailed with your settings.

If you find yourself describing all the items in a room and in such detail that the reader knows the exact shade of midnight blue fabric on the main character's two-seater duck feather stuffed, gold thread trimmed couch, you've gone *too* far.

There's nothing wrong with writing that there's a blue couch. If that's the only time the setting is mentioned, and it's not relevant to the plot, you *don't* need to channel your inner salesperson and describe the room as if your book pages are a furniture catalog.

Keep it simple unless it's really relevant to the plot, or that's the consistent style of your book/writing.

Remember the Little Things

While you don't need to go too detailed, if you want to build a good picture of the surroundings in the reader's mind, *do* remember the little things.

Floor coverings, windows, curtains, bookshelves, knick-knacks on said bookshelves. If it's a living room, it should feel lived in.

Think of all the little things that make your own home feel like home, such as a dog-eared book on a coffee table next to a steaming mug of tea, or your 7-year-old's socks left in the middle of the floor. Little things create the big picture.

Sense Everything

This is especially important when your characters are in restaurants or cooking in their kitchen. If that's your room setting, take it to the next level by remembering to add in the senses.

Describing the setting of a café becomes more authentic when your main character hears the clang of cutlery, diners chatting, drinks being poured and smells the saucy goodness of the pasta dish placed before them.

For other room settings, your character might notice the way the light filters through their window and how the brightness makes them squint.

Describe the smells, sounds, tastes, and sights of your room setting, and pair it with everything on this checklist to make it easy for your readers to immerse themselves in your book world.

Related Checklists

The Little Details Checklist
The Five Senses Checklist
The Book Openings Checklist
The What to Establish in a Scene Checklist

The Settings Checklist

◯ **Make It Authentic**
Specific details are key. Add them.

◯ **Weave It In**
Have your characters interact with their setting, not simply list what they see in a boring, paint-by-numbers description.

◯ **Make It Balanced**
If you find yourself getting bored or skipping the parts that delve into the setting too deeply, take that as a sign to pare it back.

◯ **Use Your Characters**
Filter the book settings through the eyes of each character.

◯ **Don't Describe Everything at the Start**
Spread the description throughout your scene/book, not just at the start.

 The Settings Checklist

○ **Build a Picture**
Even if it's basic, build a picture of where characters are in a scene.

○ **Avoid Sounding like a Salesperson**
Don't describe the room as if your book pages are a furniture catalog.

○ **Remember the Little Things**
Think of all the little things that make your own home feel like home and use them to create the big picture.

○ **Sense Everything**
Describe the smells, sounds, tastes, and sights of your room settings.

The POV Checklist

As a reader, there's nothing more fun than slipping wholly into the Point of View (POV) of a character. It's also creatively satisfying being a writer who can master such a skill.

Writing your book from the perspectives of your characters and getting it right forms a connection for both you and the reader, so if it's a part of your writing that you'd like to nail, here is how you can.

Run the Numbers

If you're planning to write from the POV of just one character, congratulations, your work here is done.

If you are going to write from multiple POVs then you need to decide on a number.

This involves taking a look at your cast of characters and seeing who is worthy. As talented as you might be at writing from the perspective of the shop owner the main character runs by in chapter three, if they aren't an integral part of the story, skip their POV.

- Stick to the characters who will move the plot forward and are significant.

- Don't have multiple POVs just for the sake of it.

- If a character's POV doesn't serve a purpose to the overall story, cut them and give any relevant info to another character to impart.

This number can go up and down as you write, and you might change everything three drafts in, but if you can start the first draft with a basic idea of the number of POVs you'll need, you're off to a great start.

Flag Early Changes

Once you've got the number for how many POVs you'll be using, plot when you'll change from one POV to another, and make it as early in the story as you can.

This is a lesson I learned the hard way. My series *Blackbirch* uses multiple POVs, but an early draft didn't switch from the main character's POV to another character until six chapters in and was rightly flagged by a beta reader as confusing and jarring.

- Make it clear early in your manuscript that there are *multiple* POVs by starting the second chapter with a different POV, or swap scene-by-scene from the get-go.

- Plot where your POV changes will happen as you outline so you can create the right balance (if you're a pantser and not a planner, you can do this *after* you've written the first draft).

Choose the Correct Person

Once you know how many POVs you'll need and how often you'll change them, decide on your *person*.

- When writing a POV, it's either from First Person (I), Second Person (You), or Third Person (Her, She, They).

- If you aren't sure which to go with, First and Third are usually the most popular.

- First creates a very personal POV.

- Third is written from a distance.

Check your favorite books, or books popular in your genre, if you need help making the decision, or try writing a sample chapter in First, Second, and Third and go with the one you're most comfortable writing/prefer.

Signal the Switch

If you're jumping from one character's POV to the next with no obvious signal, not only will you be mixing up your POVs and confusing the reader, you'll also be creating a head hopping mess to clean up when you edit.

- Signal your POV switch with a scene or chapter break that uses an obvious space, asterisk, or other marker, and stick to that formula.

If you do this from the first draft, you'll be thanking yourself when you're working on the fifth.

Make It Interesting

POV gives you the chance to make your characters and the story interesting.

- Everything your character sees, touches, and feels can be shown in POV, and will give them depth.

- You can use POV to add layers and twists to your story. For example, you could tell an event from one character's POV and then the same event from a different character's POV that contradicts the first. The reader will turn to the last page just to learn which version is the truth.

- Experiment with it and don't be afraid to write your scenes with different characters as the POV to see what works. It might lead to a plot breakthrough or an idea that changes the outcome of the story entirely.

- When you're switching between multiple POVs, you have the chance to leave one character's story thread open before going into a different POV on the next chapter, giving readers a mini cliffhanger where they'll keep reading until it gets back to the POV/story thread that's unresolved.

Use Knowable Knowledge

When you know the story so intimately, it's easy to overlook if you've written that a character knows something that they shouldn't.

It could be a simple slip in a piece of dialogue, an internal thought, or buried in a paragraph that you don't notice when writing, but can fix when editing by looking at events your POV character references or mentions to make sure that:

- They *are* supposed to know this information.
- This is the point of time in the story when *they do* know this information.

You'd be surprised how easy it is to miss that your main character has alluded to a conversation they had no knowledge of or that they've spoken about an event too early because your current draft doesn't accurately reflect a change in the timeline since your last edit.

Switch to Observed Thoughts and Feels

Unless your story is from the POV of an omnipresent narrator, the POV character *can't* know what the other characters are thinking.

It's an easy trap to fall into, especially for new writers. To avoid it...

- Scour your scenes for sentences where the POV mentions another character's thoughts or feelings as if they're facts and rephrase, so it's an *observation* instead.
- Ensure your POV character is observing or speculating from the tone of voice, facial expressions, or body language of the other characters, and you'll have your bases covered.

Examples:

Telling: Jenny studied Carla's face. **She was angry** about the way things had gone at the party.

Observing: Jenny studied Carla's face. **Was she angry about the way things had gone at the party?**

In the first example, the POV character of Jenny *knows* how Carla is feeling and is straight-up *telling* the reader. In the second, Jenny *questions* if Carla is angry based on her *observation* of her expression and questions it to herself, which lets *the reader assume* Carla is angry without breaking POV

It's easy to mess up, but also easy to fix.

Apply Distinct Consistency

While the style of writing across your book should be consistent, the "voice" of each character should also be distinct.

You want your readers to tell whose POV they're in just by reading the first few sentences. If your character's voice is strong, they'll be able to do that.

- Ensure your character's voice is consistent.

- If it's not, edit until every scene for said character is in *their* voice.

Eliminate Repeats

As writers, we know new ideas pop up as we're writing. Suddenly, your character having a skill like rock climbing hits you like lightning, so you mention it.

You then mention it again five chapters later, and then again before they're about to use that convenient skill in the finale to save the love of their life.

When drafting, info and emotions pop up time and time again, and if you've been drafting over a long period, you may not notice the repeated info.

- When editing, highlight any information that is mentioned more than once.

- Reduce it to the right amount of mentions (it could be anything from just once to three times at critical moments spread across the book).

- Make sure the mention/s come at the right time in the story to be a timely reminder for the reader, or to make or break a plot point.

The same rule goes for reminiscing, flashbacks, references, and memories. If you're touching on these things too much, use an editing pass to identify, refine, and eliminate.

Related Checklists

The Repeats Checklist
The Deep POV Checklist
The Head Hopping Checklist
The Internal Thoughts Checklist
The Distinct Characters Checklist

The POV Checklist

○ **Run the Numbers**
Decide on the number of POVs you're going to write from.

○ **Flag Early Changes**
Plot when you'll change from one POV to another, and make it as early in the story as possible.

○ **Choose the Correct Person**
Will you write from First Person (I), Second Person (You), or Third Person (Her, She, They)?

○ **Signal the Switch**
Mark your POV switch with a scene or chapter break using an obvious space, asterisk, or graphic.

○ **Make It Interesting**
Use the POVs to create interesting characters and story choices.

The POV Checklist

◯ **Use Knowable Knowledge**
Make sure the POV only knows what they're supposed to know at any given time.

◯ **Switch to Observed Thoughts and Feels**
Remember that the POV character can't know what the other characters are thinking or feeling, but can make observations about it to get that info to the readers.

◯ **Use Distinct Consistency**
Make it so readers can instantly tell whose POV they're in thanks to a distinct, consistent character voice.

◯ **Eliminate Repeats**
Use an editing pass to identify, refine, and eliminate repeated info, reminiscing, flashbacks, references, and memories.

The Foreshadowing Checklist

ONE OF THE BEST elements that you can add to your book is foreshadowing. This is where you drop clues so your readers don't get to that awesome plot twist and immediately think, *Where did that come from?*

In that situation, the reaction you want is *I knew it! Mind blown*, and to get it, you need this checklist.

Make It Believable

The first rule of foreshadowing is to use it believably.

Even unbelievable twists designed to turn your plot on its head benefit from this rule, because if the twists come out of nowhere, you will not get the impact you want.

- The best foreshadowing is something casual.
- Make it a mention of a character's fear in a low-key conversation, or a key item listed in their possession among other everyday items like it's no big deal. Only later does that fear or key item come into play and reveal its significance.

When doing this, you also need to give the reader some credit that they'll remember the fear or the key item, and not hit them over the head with the information. Readers are smart and they notice things, even if it's only subconsciously.

Use It for Tension

Tension is an important ingredient in a book and will keep the reader flipping those pages.

- One way to add tension is with the kind of foreshadowing that pops a little question here and there for the reader, such as why the main character wears pink on Wednesdays, or why that throwaway line of the main character's best friend not liking spicy food will come back around in unexpected ways later.

You need those little foreshadowing hooks to add the tension and to exploit the reader's need to find these things out.

Always Turn It Into a Payoff

Readers like payoffs. If something happens in your novel, they want to see it resolved—good, bad or ugly.

Foreshadowing is the same. There needs to be a reason you've mentioned that your main character spent time on a boat as a kid and knows how to tie a rope. If the foreshadowing doesn't amount to anything and you introduce all those loose threads without tying them up (either in the current book or a future book if it's part of a series), all you end up doing is frustrating the reader and complicating your story unnecessarily.

- Think of foreshadowing like a question: you've asked it, and it deserves to be answered.

Add Doubt

If you're worried that foreshadowing something and then paying it off will be boring, throw in some doubt.

That envelope slipped in the main character's mailbox with the threatening note inside looks just like the one he saw on his co-worker's desk, but it's also used throughout the entire office, including by the mail boy who knows everything about everyone and always stares your main character down.

- Foreshadow an element that can have multiple outcomes/payoffs and give your readers cause to doubt the most obvious answer.

Use doubt and you'll be using foreshadowing for one of its strongest purposes.

Don't Go Overboard

As great as foreshadowing is, like everything, too much of a good thing just doesn't work.

If you're dropping too many hints, readers will put together your reveals halfway through the book. That doesn't make it a great book for anyone.

- Ration your foreshadowing to the major twists or the ones that will have the most impact.

Foreshadowing every little thing will get tiresome, so don't go overboard with it.

Space It Out

Where you place your foreshadowing is also a craft unto itself.

You want to get it in early so it's ticking away in the reader's brain, but you don't want it so early that they forget it by the time it gets to the reveal. You also don't want to foreshadow something and then have it happen on the very next page, which will totally rob the foreshadowing of its tension.

- Find the right balance, such as foreshadowing the final chapter reveal in the first chapter, but slipping in a subtle reminder halfway through.

For example, that knife the main character put into their pocket on the fifth page accidentally nicks them on the one-hundredth, before they finally use it to escape the villain's clutches during the final chapter.

Don't Let It Overwhelm You

Knowing how great foreshadowing is and what it can do for your story can lead to some doubt about whether you can pull it off. If you're worried about foreshadowing right and it's crippling your writing process, remember that you can plant the foreshadowing any time, during any draft.

- Foreshadow *after* you've written everything and know the full plot.

That way you can work in your clues at the right places and know for sure that everything falls into place.

Types of Foreshadowing

Prophecy

This is where you tell the reader an outcome of events in the story, or what's likely regarding the destiny of your main character, using cryptic clues, fortunes, and omens.

Concrete

Basically, if you mention it—whether it's a long-lost relative, a missing trinket, a red car, or a rare book—that item/thing/person should show up and pay off their significance in another part of the story.

Symbolic

This involves no obvious clues. Instead, you'll use other elements as a symbol, such as a character who will die seeing a crow (the traditional symbol of death) before their demise.

Red Herring

Red herrings exist to throw everyone off the scent, injecting all of the mystery, surprise, suspicion, and intrigue that can be handled by your plot. Just about anything can be a red herring.

Flashback/Flashforward

Use flashbacks or flashforwards (or even flashsideways if you're going the *Lost* route) to tell readers relevant info that doesn't happen in the current storyline.

Related Checklists

The Tension Checklist
The Payoff Checklist
The Assumptions Checklist

The Foreshadowing Checklist

◯ **Types of Foreshadowing**
Select the correct type or types of foreshadowing to use in your story from the common options, such as Prophecy, Concrete, Symbolic, Red Herring, Flashback/Flashforward.

◯ **Make It Believable**
Use casual mentions and believability to insert your foreshadowing in a way that doesn't hit the reader over the head with obviousness.

◯ **Use It for Tension**
Pop a little question here and there for the reader that will later come back around in unexpected ways.

◯ **Always Turn It Into a Payoff**
There needs to be a reason you've mentioned the foreshadowing and it should always be resolved/explained.

The Foreshadowing Checklist

◯ **Add Doubt**
Foreshadow something with multiple outcomes/payoffs and give your readers cause to doubt the most obvious answer.

◯ **Don't Go Overboard**
Ration your foreshadowing to the major twists or the ones that will have the most impact.

◯ **Space It Out**
Foreshadow the final chapter reveal in the first chapter, but slip in a subtle reminder halfway through.

◯ **Don't Let It Overwhelm You**
Foreshadow after you've written the full plot to work your clues into the right places.

The Plot Twist Checklist

Is THERE ANYTHING AS good as reading a story and coming across a plot twist so great it completely blows you away?

When done right, a plot twist will turn a tale on its head, get readers flipping pages, and talking about your work to anyone who'll listen. If that sounds like something you want in your manuscript, this checklist is for you.

Come Up with a Twist

Some plot twists happen as you're writing. You didn't plan it; you didn't see it coming, and you are the first reader to be surprised by the twist.

When it happens organically in the writing process, it should read that way in the finished draft. If you're not sure, have a beta reader check that the twist is a natural fit in the story, and then thank your muse/writing-brain for coming up with something so genius.

If an unplanned twist hasn't manifested in your rough drafts, then you've got some planning to do, and in some ways, that's even more fun.

To create a planned twist, look at...

- Every incident.
- Character interactions.
- The overall plot.

And study where and when to drop in a twist that will elevate your story to the next level.

It may take countless notebook pages, and a little of your sanity, but if you do the twist right, it will be worth it.

Brainstorming is a great way to do this. You can even brainstorm an organically created twist and see if you can make it better.

- Get yourself a piece of paper or a new digital document.
- Jot down every idea you can think of that will add a twist to your plot.
- Forget anything that's way too simple, that'll only create something the readers will see coming.
- Keep any idea that has merit and expand on it.
- What else can you do to the twist?
- What are two outcomes that could happen?
- Ask yourself all those crazy "What-if?" questions and see where you land.

Somewhere in there is your plot twist, and once you have the idea, you just need to finesse it.

Add Red Herrings

No plot twist is complete without a red herring to throw it off track. This is when you purposely misdirect the reader.

- Red herrings should be plausible and entertaining.
- You want to distract the reader with a red herring they're invested in enough to follow, but not be too disappointed by when they realize it's a misdirect.
- Don't lie to readers or plant a clue that goes nowhere (you don't want to be *that* writer).

The red herring might not be what the reader thought it would be, but it should still have a purpose.

Know Where to Place Clues

For a good twist to work, you need clues the reader can pick up on, but ones that aren't so obvious the twist is guessed as soon as the first clue is planted.

It's a tricky balance to get right. You might be tempted to drop a clue on the second page that doesn't pay off until the final, but that's a risky game. It could take a reader months to get through your book, and that early clue could be long forgotten.

- Try to work your clue, or a subtle reminder of it, into the twist's vicinity.

- Another good way to drop a hint without it being obvious is during a big scene.

Say you have two characters fighting, heated words are said, and the tension is thick. There's so much going on, the reader is glued to the page. They're so invested they don't notice that one little clue dropped in a slip of a character's tongue, or that an important item is knocked astray when the main character storms out of the room.

The twist clue is simply absorbed into the reader's subconscious and lost to the chapter's action. Then, when the twist finally hits, the seed you planted when they were focused on other things has its time to bloom.

Don't Forget to Foreshadow

Your readers saying *"Now it all makes perfect sense!"* is the highest of honors after you've dropped your twist. The way to achieve that is to...

- Foreshadow the twist.

Let's consider an example where there's a murder victim and the key to solving their death is on a password-protected USB drive. One twist in the story is that the password is the opening line of the victim's favorite song. If that song was never mentioned before the twist, it all falls flat when the info is revealed.

The reader might see it as coming out of nowhere or not consider it a big deal. If instead, that song twist is *foreshadowed* in a flashback or a conversation before the main character died, suddenly the twist is more exciting. The reader was aware of the song already and it now feels like a puzzle piece has slipped into place.

Steer Clear of Cheap Tricks

Cheap tricks are the kind of things that make a reader stop reading or throw your book across the room when they're done.

- Don't go for cheap tricks like the twist being a dream or an evil twin.
- Unless you're pulling off something fresh with these clichés, keep them out of your plot twists.

You want readers to tell others about your book, remember? And you want them doing it because you had a plot twist that was fresh, made sense in the story, didn't get bogged down in an unsatisfying red herring, and was foreshadowed perfectly with the best-placed clues.

Related Checklists

The Reverse Outlining Checklist
The Unpredictability Checklist
The Foreshadowing Checklist
The Payoff Checklist

 The Plot Twist Checklist

◯ **Come Up with a Twist**
Look at incidents, interactions, and the overall plot to brainstorm a twist.

◯ **Add Red Herrings**
Purposely misdirect the reader from the twist with something that's plausible, has a purpose, and is entertaining.

◯ **Know Where to Place Clues**
Leave clues near the twist vicinity and drop hints while something big is also happening so the twist isn't too obvious from the first clue.

◯ **Don't Forget to Foreshadow**
Plant clues about the twist before it happens via flashbacks or conversations.

◯ **Steer Clear of Cheap Tricks**
Avoid typical twist clichés unless you're pulling off something fresh.

The Info-Dumping Checklist

IF YOU HAVEN'T HEARD of it before, info-dumping is when the writer bombards the reader with everything they think they should know—*all at once*.

While you might think there's no way *you* do that, info-dumping is an easy trap to fall into. It's one of those author blind spots we can easily see in other's work, but don't in our own.

It worms its way in like typos, but here are some likely places you'll find info-dumping, so you can use this checklist to avoid it.

Check the Starts

Info-dumping likes to live at the start of things, such as...

- The first chapter.
- The first introduction of a character.
- The first instance of world-building.

It sets up home there because the writer makes it the perfect place to build.

Think about what happens when you're penning the first draft. You're discovering the story, telling it to yourself, and getting it all on the page. Once it's there, we forget to examine it in later drafts for info-dumping.

As an example, let's say it's the first time your main character has visited the place your story is set. Trying to work out where you were going with it, your writer-brain brought in another character with a lengthy explanation of the town's history and why no one goes near the creepy abandoned two-story house on Cliché Crescent.

You had to know those things to move onto your next chapter, but it's likely the reader *doesn't* need to on their first read. The story could be much more interesting if the weird town is revealed in layers instead.

So, mention that it's a weird place when the main character arrives, but hint at the rest. The background of the house on Cliché Crescent can come later when it will have an impact instead of being lost in an info-dump.

With that tip in mind, check every place in your WIP where you introduce...

- A character.
- A setting.
- A nugget of knowledge.

And see how it can be split into *one* tantalizing drop of info, with the rest to follow later. You'll be avoiding an info-dump, and creating plenty of intrigue to keep the reader turning those pages.

Manage the Monologuing

A monologue can really make or break a scene. It's a good way to reveal things, remind the reader of events, and show off your dialogue skills, but it's also a very easy place to dump your info.

The villain monologue is a classic example. Here you have the enemy of your main character—mostly likely sitting in a chair patting a cat—while they lay out their evil plan. They think they're smart. They usually end it with an evil laugh, satisfied that they've gotten the better of everyone. More like *bored* everyone.

Monologuing all of your info is *not* the way to keep the reader entertained. Manage it instead by...

- Getting the info across in a back-and-forth battle between your villain and hero, revealing the info as they trade barbs between blows.

If all the info has to be known at a specific point in your novel, get it in, just not all at once in a speech that wouldn't happen in real life. A *James Bond* villain might not approve of your methods, but readers will.

Drip It in and Stretch It Out

As mentioned already, info-dumping usually arises in the first draft. The best thing about second drafts is that you can use them to rearrange those dumps and move them elsewhere.

- Look at each scene and highlight any big blocks of info.
- Once you know what the info is, break it up into smaller parts.
- Look for the places where you can drip it in and stretch it out across the book.

Treating your info like this rather than dumping it all in one place will add suspense and tension to your story—which is something every good read needs.

Fine-Tune the Dialogue

Similar to monologuing, info-dumping in your dialogue is when your characters are having a conversation just to get the info across. It's usually stilted and wraps up once the right info is imparted.

- To reveal info in dialogue without it being a dump, fine-tune it so it's a natural part of the conversation.

It should effortlessly fit in with what's happening in the scene.

Make It Relevant

Just like dumpy dialogue that sticks out like a sore thumb, if you're putting your info in places it's not needed, or during scenes where more important things are happening, you risk pulling the reader from the story.

Let's go back to our example of the main character in the weird town with the abandoned house. He's heard the rumors and wants to test them for himself.

Now, in the abandoned house on Cliché Crescent, he finds a dark basement. He's creeping down the stairs, strange noises assaulting his ears, nothing in front of him but pitch-black, and he decides to info-dump the history of the house he's learned or some background about how he's hated basements since he was a kid after accidentally being locked in one.

Is any of that relevant for the character and story? *Yes*. Could you work it in at a different time and *not* when all the creepy action is taking place? *Yes*. And you should.

Don't ruin the read with irrelevant info-dumping. Don't halt the momentum of a chase scene by stopping to describe the surroundings. Check your...

- Intense scenes.

- Action chapters.

- Emotional arcs that are about to pay off.

- Plot points ready to twist.

And don't weigh *any* of them down with big chunks of info. Put that info in other relevant places in the story instead.

By following this advice, the reader will know more about the story and your characters, but *not* at the cost of your pacing.

Related Checklists

The Book Openings Checklist
The Dialogue Tips Checklist
The Plot Twist Checklist
The Scene Isn't Working Checklist

The Info-Dumping Checklist

☐ Check the Starts
Eliminate/reduce your info-dumping from the following firsts:
- First chapter.
- First introduction of a character.
- First instance of world-building.
- First instance of a book setting.

☐ Manage the Monologuing
Get the info across in a back-and-forth battle/conversation between characters rather than a one-sided long monologue.

☐ Drip It in and Stretch It Out
When possible, scatter your info across the book.
- Highlight any big blocks of info.
- Break the info into smaller parts and drip it into the scenes, and/or stretch it out across the whole book.

☐ Fine-Tune the Dialogue
Make info-dumps in conversations a natural part of the dialogue rather than something stilted that wraps up unnaturally once the info is spilled.

☐ Make It Relevant
Avoid adding info in places where more important things are happening, i.e. don't halt the momentum of a chase scene by stopping to describe the surroundings.

The Conflict Checklist

When penning a story, there are a few essential ingredients to add to the mix, and one of them is conflict.

This is because humans love drama. That's the reason reality TV shows are *still* around and why readers enjoy stories that use conflict to hold their interest.

Does that mean your book needs to be filled with back-stabbing scenarios and crazy plot twists? *No* (although if that's the book you want to write, go for it!).

Conflict does *not* have to be over-the-top. Quiet conflict, the kind a character internally wrestles with, can be just as entertaining when done right, so try sprinkling it and other types of conflict in with the help of this checklist.

Take Away Character Wants/Needs

A classic case of conflict is taking something important from your character.

If they need a certain grade to get into school, have them fail. If they live for their child, what would happen if they were separated?

- Think about how you would feel if something essential for your life was ripped away and channel it into your words.

When your main character has to fight for what they want/need, the conflict is guaranteed, so do as much taking as you can.

Pile on the Consequences

A character who wins all the time gets stale quickly, but a character who has consequences for their wins is one that maintains interest.

If you want that kind of factor in your story...

- Take a look at your events and make sure you've included consequences—good and bad—for your characters and their actions.

The more consequences you have, the more it could lead to other issues, which will only compound that conflict, automatically upping the interest.

Create Flawed Characters

A well-rounded character is a flawed character and you can use those flaws to inject conflict into your story.

- Give your character something to achieve.

- Throw everything at them to mess it up.

A huge promotion after a year of hard work could see your main character realize they aren't cut out for their new role. Whether they sink with their shortcomings or rise above them and become better is a story readers love to follow—all thanks to conflict.

Make Things Personal

How many books have you read and movies have you seen that really kicked off once something personal happened to the main character? I'm going to say a fair few because that's good storytelling.

When something is personal for a character, they will go to the ends of the earth, betray their nearest and dearest, rob a bank, and/or sacrifice themselves. After all, *John Wick* didn't massacre his way through multiple movies for *no* reason. They killed his dog.

- Give your main character something personal to win or lose.

It forces them to act or do something, usually outlandish, leaving the conflict to create itself.

Cram Them Between a Rock and a Hard Place

Conflict works because it's usually nothing good. If you want to amp that up, put your character between the proverbial rock and a hard place.

- Give them lose-lose situations.

Things such as deciding if their spouse dies at the cost of their child. Yes, it's cruel and a grim decision, but it's also conflict gold.

Readers will be on the edge wondering how things will pan out, and if they'd do the same in a similar situation. They'll also keep reading to find out.

Disrupt the Status Quo

Is your character living their best life? Are they happy in their dream job, or in their relationship? Did they just get the house they wanted, or marry their first love? If so, change it.

- Disrupt every normal thing in their life.
- Upend the status quo.

Family secrets, deception, underhanded work by a colleague—almost anything can be changed from the usual to something left of field, fueling everything that happens to your character with, you guessed it, conflict.

Isolate the Main Character

While we could all do with a little me-time now and then, isolation that is extreme and ongoing is*n't* ideal.

Nobody does well in such situations, and neither would your main character.

- Take away their support system, either via circumstance, the actions of an antagonist, or from the character's own choices.

Not only will you create conflict, but it could be what turns your book into a must-read.

That's the power of compelling conflict and why making it an essential part of your story will benefit your book.

Related Checklists

The Character Motivation Checklist
The Tension Checklist

The Conflict Checklist

◯ **Take Away Character Wants/Needs**
When your main character has to fight for what they want/need, the conflict is guaranteed, so do as much taking as you can.

◯ **Pile on the Consequences**
Include consequences—good and bad—for your characters and their actions in your book events.

◯ **Create Flawed Characters**
Whether they sink with their shortcomings, or rise above them and become better, is a story readers love to follow.

◯ **Make Things Personal**
Give your main character something personal to win or lose so they act outlandishly to correct the situation.

◯ **Cram Them Between a Rock and a Hard Place**
Give your characters impossible, lose-lose situations, such as deciding if their spouse dies at the cost of their child.

◯ **Disrupt the Status Quo**
Almost anything can be changed from the usual to something left of field, fueling what happens to your character with conflict.

◯ **Isolate the Main Character**
Take away your character's support system using circumstance, the actions of an antagonist, or the character's own choices.

The Unpredictability Checklist

WHEN YOU THINK OF a compelling read, the fact you couldn't see any of the twists and turns coming is probably one reason why you couldn't put the book down.

Unpredictability is a fun feature to come across as a reader, and something any writer will benefit from in their own work, and here is how you can add it.

Double Down on the Doubt

Making your readers doubt a character's motives, actions, or the truth in a story can make your book a page-turner. How to take it to an unpredictable level is to double down on that doubt.

As an example, imagine that you've hinted at the actual killer, dropped everything on the most obvious suspect, but also left some doubt about if it's really them by focusing things on a side character too.

The reader thinks they have it all worked out until the closing chapters where you double that doubt and suddenly everything points to your main character being the true villain!

No reader will know where the story is going after that and you've most likely blown their minds.

If you'd love that outcome for your own tome...

- Brainstorm how to add doubt into your scenes.

- Work out how you can turn it on its head for an extra dose of uncertainty.

Play Into the Familiar Before Flipping It

When you set up your story or characters familiarly, readers will play into those known tropes and stereotypes and predict exactly where you're going with your story.

It's a blessing, as in it gives readers what they expect and want, but also a curse because when it plays out like they know it will, you've got no unpredictability.

There is a way around that, however, and that's flipping those known things.

- Make things very familiar and then add something unpredictable/twisty.
- Make sure to ingeniously foreshadow it so that your clichéd familiar moves are flipped on their head.

Make your story full of predictability until it's not and leave an impression on any audience.

Give Everyone What They Deserve (The Good and the Bad)

One predictable thing that readers love to see in a story is the hero scrapping through the battle triumphantly, and the villain getting their comeuppance. But what if the hero deserves some punishment too?

Sometimes our main character, even if they are the star of the story, does gray area stuff. No human is perfect, and well-rounded characters have flaws.

- If your main character has done something that deserves repercussions, don't ignore it.
- Don't get them out of it and act as if everything is sunshine and rainbows because the hero always wins.

Your reader will expect that, just as they expect the antagonist to lose. But if everyone has been bad, they all deserve what's coming for them.

On the flip side, an antagonist who can't foil the main character as predicted could find themselves with an unpredictable win. Their scheming ways may have seen them miss out on being valedictorian, but coming off second-best may lead to something even better for them.

Readers won't see a win for the antagonist coming, so don't just play into the predictability of everyone getting whatever good or bad ending they deserve and leave it at that.

Take things a step further.

- See how both a fail and a victory can play out for every character and work that into your story.

It won't be something a reader is expecting and may deliver a more satisfying end to your story thanks to the unpredictability.

Related Checklists

The Plot Twist Checklist
The Foreshadowing Checklist
The Assumptions Checklist

# The Unpredictability Checklist

○ **Double Down on the Doubt**
Work doubt into your scenes and then turn it on its head for an extra dose of uncertainty.

○ **Play Into the Familiar Before Flipping It**
Make things familiar and then add something unpredictable/twisty.

○ **Give Everyone What They Deserve**
See how both a failure and a victory can play out for every character and work that into your story to keep the reader on their toes.

The Head Hopping Checklist

HEAD HOPPING IS AN issue that can crop up when writing in third POV, and involves placing the reader inside the head of one or more characters within the same scene. Why is this bad? Well, for starters, it's confusing.

Jumping from one character's inner thoughts to another within close paragraphs and sentences makes it difficult for a reader to keep track of who is thinking and feeling what.

To ensure you don't do this, this checklist will help you find and eliminate head hopping from your writing.

Pick a POV Character and Stick With Them

Whatever scene or chapter you are in, it should be from *one* character's point of view (POV), and that point of view only.

Obviously, there can be other characters in the scene, interacting with the POV character, but everything from...

- How the setting looks, feels, smells.
- Internal reactions to what is happening in the scene.

Should only filter through to the reader via the POV character.

Switching from the main character describing their shock at seeing a person hit by a car, to side character #2 describing how the same event is making them feel nauseous, means that you've head hopped.

Staying in the head of the POV character but *showing externally* how a different character reacts can be done without that head hopping, and that's when you opt for the next tip—distance tricks.

Employ Distance Tricks

Since your POV is from one character, you need to use them to relay everyone else's reactions.

Because you can't directly show what the other characters' internal thoughts are or what they're feeling via their heads...

- Use the POV character's observation skills.
- They can tell the reader the mood of another character via dialogue, actions, and what the POV character sees and hears.

As an example, our POV character, Carla, asks the other character, Jenny, to help her move a large box.

Example:

Carla nudged the box with the tip of her sneaker. "Jenny, can you help me with this?"
Her friend's gaze narrowed on the box's size, and Jenny crossed her arms. "That's a little too big, don't you think?"
It was too big for Carla by herself, but surely, with Jenny's help, she could bring it inside. "If you just grab the other end, we can pick it up."
"Ugh." Jenny stomped over, kicking the box with her shoe, before letting out a sigh.

In this simple example, Jenny didn't want to help and was annoyed by the size of the box. Instead of hopping into Jenny's head to show this to the reader, we use the POV of Carla to get the same info across.

This is done via what *she* sees, such as Jenny's gaze narrowing at the box, crossing her arms, and Jenny stomping over. Jenny's annoyance is further displayed by what Carla can hear in Jenny's dialogue, and with Jenny's sigh at the end.

Just remember...

- The viewpoint character can tell you everything they're seeing, thinking, and feeling.

- Other characters need to show it via dialogue and audible cues like grunts and sighs, and with physical manifestations, such as jumping up and down to show they're excited.

Another way to make the most of distance tricks is by having your POV character observe or hear an outside source.

- A news report blasting from a TV in a café.

- A blog headline flashing on their phone screen.

- A cryptic conversation overheard on the train during the morning commute.

All these methods work just as well without you having to pop inside the head of another character.

Use the Highlight Method

If you've already written your book and weren't keeping track of head hopping, or are now paranoid that you've done it, you can check your text using the highlight method.

This involves getting your hands on some different highlight colors (either digitally or physically if you're working from a printed copy) and assigning one color to the POV character.

With that specific color...

- Highlight their name.

- Highlight everything in your words that points to them being the POV character, such as statements like:

- She saw.

- She heard.

- She felt.

- She needed.

- She knew.

- Internal thoughts and observations.

Read the rest of the text again and look closely at the sentences around the other characters in the scene.

- If you can use another highlight color to mark POV statements from *anyone else*, you've head hopped, and the scene needs to be rewritten.

While you might think head hopping isn't one of the worst writer sins to commit, or that plenty of classic books pull it off, know that they've mastered the rules and broken them. It's likely you're not in that league yet, and eliminating head hopping will only benefit your book.

Besides taking out the confusion, no head hopping means more of an emotional impact for your scenes. Your readers get that by bonding with your POV character.

If you're switching from one character's head to another in quick succession, they can't connect with your POV character, and without that connection, they won't follow them to the last page or the next book.

Related Checklists

The POV Checklist
The Internal Thoughts Checklist
The Dialogue Tips Checklist

The Head Hopping Checklist

◯ **Pick a POV Character and Stick With Them**
Whatever the scene, everything should be filtered from one character's point of view only.

◯ **Employ Distance Tricks**
Use the POV character's observation skills to relay the mood/actions of others, and have them observe or hear relevant info from outside sources, such as a blog headline flashing on their phone screen.

◯ **Use the Highlight Method**
Check your text with a highlighter to mark the POV character and highlight their:
- Internal thoughts.
- Observations.
- POV statements (she saw/heard/felt/needed/knew).

The same type of text coming from a different character within the same scene is head hopping and needs to be removed.

The Assumptions Checklist

IF YOU'RE CREATING A page-turner, one writing trick to get on your side is an assumption.

An assumption allows readers to fill in what they *think* is happening with their own experiences. If the reader believes they've figured out what's going on, and the truth leads them in a different direction, you've most likely gained a fan for life.

This is exactly what you want when crafting a great story, and this checklist will allow you to add all of the assumptions that your plot allows.

Dual It Up

To successfully pull off an assumption, you'll want to play into it, but if you want to make it twist-worthy as well...

- Give the assumption a dual meaning.

An example of this can be found in the 2011 movie *Crazy, Stupid, Love*. In it, Steve Carell's character, Cal Weaver, is going through a marriage breakdown and mentions not wanting "Nana" to find out.

"Nana" being a common name for a grandmother, means the audience assumes he is referring to his grandmother. They believe this until the end of the movie when it's revealed that "Nana" is actually the nickname of his grown daughter, Hannah, a character viewers didn't know until that point was even related to Cal.

The dual-ness of "Nana" being an obvious name for Cal's grandmother, but in reality, the plausible nickname of Hannah is what makes this assumption work, and this is something you can pull off in your writing too.

To try it...

- Subtly lead the reader toward an obvious assumption that also has a dual meaning with a plausible truth.

Not only will you trump expectations, but the actual truth could create a crafty plot twist, a sad new truth, a sober dose of reality, or a joyful surprise.

Play With Foreshadowed Misunderstandings

Another way to make the most of an assumption is to...

- Create misunderstandings until the real truth comes out.

- Foreshadow those misunderstandings.

Let's say that you have an main character who has been cheated on in the past. This history can be mentioned as she's with a friend, getting ready to go to a party, and lending said friend a bracelet the main character doesn't wear much because it always slips off.

Now, the party is being held by the main character's new boyfriend, who she has so far had a good, trusting relationship with. After being greeted by the new boyfriend and asked to put their coats in his room, the main character and her friend enjoy their night. Later, the main character gets separated from her boyfriend for a length of time and also loses track of her friend.

Remember, she's been cheated on in the past, and while trying to ignore her creeping paranoia, the main character eventually finds her friend. Before leaving, the main character ducks into the boyfriend's room to grab her coat, and finds the bracelet she lent her friend on the bedside table.

With the cheating history foreshadowed, the main character (and the reader) makes the obvious assumption. She knows the bracelet is hers and that her friend was wearing it. The same friend she'd lost track of at the same time as her boyfriend. With these assumptions, the reader is now just as ready as the main character to declare war on the cheating friend and boyfriend.

But what else was foreshadowed? The bracelet was prone to falling off. That's why the main character rarely wore it, and the boyfriend told the girls to put their coats in his room. Isn't it likely that the slippery bracelet fell off when the friend was putting away her coat, and someone else getting their own coat found it on the floor and put it on the bedside table? *Yes, it is*. But the assumption and foreshadowing played their part first, giving drama to the plot and taking the reader where the writer wanted them to go.

If that bracelet had slipped off in the kitchen during the party, the main character and the reader wouldn't have jumped to the conclusion of an affair, but with the right foreshadowing of cheating and the location for the assumption, this writer's trick was pulled off.

Let the Characters Lead Part of the Way

One key element of assumptions that will also benefit you is your reader believing them. And they will if the characters do.

In our cheating example, until the truth is provided, the main character really thinks her friend and new boyfriend are having an affair.

In her eyes, the evidence is there, and she's made up her mind. On the page, she would have gotten to this paranoid point through the internal thoughts the reader is also in on. These character-led assumptions bring the reader to the same conclusions—but only do this to a certain point.

- Don't put every single assumption in ink. It robs the reader of the fun of making their own.

- Creating assumptions for themselves gets the reader invested in the story, so aim to lead for part of the way, and then allow readers to piece together the rest.

When those kinds of assumptions are combined with dual meanings and foreshadowing, you're on track for a *I didn't see that coming* instead of the dreaded *I don't understand/hate that*.

That's the result that you want from this fun writing trick, so assume away and see where it takes your characters and readers.

Related Checklists

The Unpredictability Checklist
The Foreshadowing Checklist

The Assumptions Checklist

○ **Dual It Up**
Subtly lead the reader in the direction of an obvious assumption that also has a dual meaning with a plausible truth.

○ **Play With Foreshadowed Misunderstandings**
Create misunderstandings until the real truth comes out and foreshadow those misunderstandings.

○ **Let the Characters Lead Part of the Way**
The reader will believe assumptions if the characters do too, but also let the reader piece together their own by not putting every assumption on the page.

The Coincidences Checklist

SOMETHING NEW FOR YOUR writing bag of tricks is coincidences (which is joincidences with a C for all you *Friends* fans).

While some writing advice will tell you to steer clear of using them too much or even altogether, they can be a powerful tool when done correctly, and this checklist will show you what to do with coincidences, as well as what pitfalls to avoid.

Don't Use Them for Convenience

If you want to avoid your readers rolling their eyes, which I think most of us do, you'll want to...

- Give the convenient coincidence a miss.

A convenient coincidence occurs when your main character runs into the very person they need at the right moment, or the file they need to keep their job hitting their desk seconds before the big meeting.

While crossing paths with the right person, or getting the right file can happen in your story, if they happen *way too easily* via a convenient coincidence rather than your main character working hard to make those things a reality, you're robbing the reader of a more interesting story.

Coincidences that cause problems are plausible. Coincidences that are conveniently helpful are not.

Do Foreshadow

Is it a coincidence that your girl-scout-in-her-youth main character has been left for dead in the woods but has all the tools to survive? Sure. But you can take that coincidence and make it work by foreshadowing her history of skills *before* she's left to fight for her life. When it doesn't work is if you only announce those handy skills when the main character uses them.

- Foreshadow the right info early to eliminate a coincidence that will put your reader in an annoyed state of disbelief.

If the audience knows ahead of time that your hero has survival skills, it's going to come across as something falling into place. That's a better option than your reader refusing to finish the book because it became unbelievable when the woods-stranded main character knew *exactly* how to combine the bark of one tree with the crushed flowers of another to make a paste to starve off infection when nothing in her prior actions or backstory pointed to such knowledge.

Don't Forget the Credibility

For certain elements of your story, the main character needs to earn what they're finding/solving/learning, and the wrong coincidences can ruin that.

Let's say, for example, that your main character learns a vital clue via an overheard conversation where they are in the right place at the right time. Such coincidences happen, but isn't it more credible that they find that info through their own hard work instead of overhearing it?

An even worse coincidence cliché is blind luck getting your characters in and out of every situation. Add credibility with...

- Earned, layered solutions to any reveals.
- By not relying on easy coincidences.

Do Get Rid of the Random Know-It-All

If you're relying on the answer to the main character's conundrum being solved by a person who enters the story via a well-placed coincidence, *please don't*.

- An expert in a certain field that the main character had to risk their life to get to giving them the right info—*yes!*
- A main character broken down on the highway and picked up by a random trucker who dabbles in learning every topic known to man while hauling freight knows the right info—*no!*

It's too coincidental, too know-it-all, and *not* good enough.

Don't Have Bumbling Bad Guys

Nobody can root for a main character who triumphs because bumbling bad guys make a stupid mistake, or ruin their own plans with a coincidence that doesn't work in their favor. It isn't a real win.

In fact, if you look at your climax and the bad guys get defeated with no real input from the main character, not only are your bad guys *the worst*, but the main character having no real impact on the outcome of the story is a letdown for the reader too.

- The protagonist needs to defeat the antagonist.
- If bumbling bad guys are creating coincidences to do the heavy lifting—reassess.

Do Steer Clear of Nicks of Time

Did the main character arrive in the nick of time to prevent the colossal explosion, even though getting from one side of the city to the other should have taken 5 hours?

It's okay, a helicopter flown by an old friend of the main character's father who was never mentioned until the sound of helicopter blades cut through the beeping horns of the grid-locked traffic arrived—*in the nick of time*—to pick our hero up and get her where she needed to be.

There are better ways to use coincidences, tension, and to stop the colossal explosion, so try them first.

- Steer clear or scale back your nick of time coincidences.

Don't Shy Away from Plausibility

Some coincidences you need, such as the new co-worker of your main character being an old crush.

Now that they're working together, there's a reason for them to cross paths and reconnect. If you instead have your main character bump into their old crush at random on the street, it lacks plausibility.

While that scenario works, and is the start of multiple rom-coms, having the main character and crush reconnect at work gives more to the story. Now they can get to know each other again during shifts until the romance blooms.

- Use plausible coincidences, not just random coincidences.

It's an investment in character relationships and makes more sense for them to be in each other's lives again instead of just a random coincidence bringing them together. By playing into the plausibility of the good coincidence of their shared history instead, you give yourself another coincidence option to mine.

Related Checklists

The Unpredictability Checklist
The Foreshadowing Checklist
The Distinct Characters Checklist

The Coincidences Checklist

☐ **Don't Use Them for Convenience**
If things happen too easily via a convenient coincidence rather than your main character working hard, you're robbing the reader of a more interesting story.

☐ **Do Foreshadow**
Include the right info early enough to eliminate a coincidence that will put your reader in an annoyed state of disbelief.

☐ **Don't Forget the Credibility**
The main character should earn what they're finding/solving/learning, and the wrong coincidences/blind luck can ruin that.

☐ **Do Get Rid of the Random Know-It-All**
Using a know-it-all character introduced only to impart the right answer is not good enough.

☐ **Don't Have Bumbling Bad Guys**
If bumbling bad guys are creating coincidences to do the heavy lifting or stopping the protagonist from defeating the antagonist—reassess.

☐ **Do Steer Clear of Nicks of Time**
Scale back your nick of time coincidences. There are better ways to use coincidences, tension, and to stop the colossal explosion, so try them first.

☐ **Don't Shy Away from Plausibility**
Use plausible coincidences, not just random coincidences, as an investment in character relationships.

The World-Building Checklist

REGARDLESS OF WHETHER YOUR story uses a world full of fantasy-filled adventures or one as mundane as our own, there's an art to world-building.

And it's an art that can be overwhelming for writers who've never created a world before, or for writer's attempting their biggest yet—such as a foray into a book series.

But world-building will benefit any story, no matter the genre, so don't shy away. You can make it as big or as small as your creativity allows. Just start with these basics.

Real World Versus Made Up

The first rule of world-building is deciding where it's set.

- Are you going to root your book in the real world or make it up?
- Once you've decided, carry it throughout your planning and story.
- With real world rules, some of the work is done for you. The reader knows how that world works because they live in it, too.
- With a fantasy world, you can be more creative and establish the rules.
- You can also combine the two and have a real-life setting mixed with fantasy elements.

In these cases, the rules of the world should be on the page so the reader knows exactly how it works.

Question Everything

After establishing the kind of world you want, it's time to question everything.

Make a list like the one below and add your answers. You may not use every detail, but the list is a good starting point to get your ideas flowing and your subconscious thinking about your world on a deeper level. That will hopefully then reflect in your world as you write.

- What does the world look like? What's the landscape? Is it a desert, underwater, a jungle? What are the special rules of those places?

- What's the language that's spoken? Is there more than one?

- What's the technology like? Do robots rule? Is there no technology? Is there advanced technology?

- Is there a magic system? Is it used by everyone, only a select few, as currency, to grant wishes? Is it illegal or very rare?

- What are the rules of society? Is it a peaceful world? Are there different tiers of people?

- Who is in charge of society? Is there a government?

- What are the systems of law?

- Is the world set on earth, in space, or on another planet?

Give the World a Backstory

Just as your characters become deeper with the help of a backstory, so can your story world.

- Plot how the world started.

- Work out how it runs.

- What would the world be like if there has never been a war?

- What differences would that make to the story and the characters?

- Would it be a peaceful society?

- Would this create an arrogant, nothing-will-ever-go-wrong society?

The backstory included in your world-building can enrich your book, spark ideas, and influence your character traits, so put some research into it and reap the benefits.

Sharpen the Details

If you're worried the world-building will overtake things, there's no rule that says you need to know or explain every little thing.

- Select details done well are enough to create a memorable or unique world.

- The world is yours to create and only needs to be as in-depth as needed to do your book justice.

- Don't feel pressured to create a world as expansive as Tolkien because you've written a fantasy series.

Your own unique ideas on a few fantasy elements might be all you need, so get the details right, but don't get dragged down by them.

Add Your Spin

This is where the tried and true *"write what you know"* advice comes in handy. When setting up your world, set it up like yours.

- Describe the main character's house like the one you grew up in.

- Make the town the dream place you'd love to live one day with all your future writing royalties (we can dream, right?)

- Write about the places you've lived and worked to add a realistic spin.

Cramped office spaces full of florescent lighting and workers divided into little cubicles might be an office cliché, but if you've worked for a faceless corporation pushing papers, you know that it's accurate. So will readers, so infuse your story world with your own world.

Cue up Some Contrasts

Contrasts in a fictional world not only help establish the settings and rules but also give your characters something to fight for or against.

Let's use *The Hunger Games* as an example. Katniss lives in a desolate district where she once survived on discarded burnt bread. When she goes to the Capitol as part of the games, there's so much food it's wasted by the rich who live there. The difference between these two levels of society helps fuel her fire to fight and gives the reader a clear contrast between the societies in *The Hunger Games* world.

- Add contrasts into your world-building to clue the reader in on how things work, motivate characters, and to add elements of depth and tension.

Set the Rules and Break Them

Just as the '90s horror classic *Scream* established the rules to live by if you wanted to survive a scary movie, your world should have its own set of rules.

They can relate to how characters live, interact, and die. Or how magic systems, law, or the environment works.

- Create your rules.
- Establish them on the page.
- Break them for a good reason, and always with a hint before the change.

Like all things, rules can be broken. If you're going to break the rules you've set out, however, there must be a reason. It should also be foreshadowed. If you don't let the reader know the rules can be changed before changing them, they'll get frustrated, and no writer wants frustrated readers.

Don't Get Trapped

This world-building basic works for standalone books, but is also an essential must-do for those crafting a book series.

World-building really shines as part of a series. Across multiple books, you have the time to establish the world and bring in all the rules without overwhelming the reader.

In an *ideal* reality, the world will be established and you'll know how everything fits across the whole series. In a *realistic* reality, you'll be writing the series across years and releasing one book at a time.

It's a system that's ripe for getting trapped by the rules you've created. What worked in book one might cause issues in book four when you've realized you've written yourself into a corner.

To work around it.

- Don't release until you've written everything, which has its own advantages and disadvantages.

- Learn to keep track of every single detail.

- Use a series bible.

- Don't rely on your own memory of what you've done. Your writer-brain remembers everything, including ideas you noted but never added, and the things you cut out.

- If books from your series have already been published and you're working on the latest installment, reread the released books.

- Write down the *actual* rules, *not* the ones from draft nine that were scrapped and only live on in your head.

- Follow the published world-building so you can keep everything cohesive.

If it's too late, use your series bible to help you add a plot twist so brilliant it looks like you knew what you were doing all along.

Related Checklists

The Settings Checklist
The Backstory Checklist
The Little Details Checklist

The World-Building Checklist

◯ **Real World Versus Made Up**
Decide if your book is set in the real world or one you are going to make up.

◯ **Question Everything**
Make a list of questions about the workings of your world (or use the ones in the expanded checklist) to get your ideas flowing and your subconscious thinking about your world on a deeper level.

◯ **Give the World a Backstory**
Use a world backstory to enrich your book.

◯ **Sharpen the Details**
You don't need to know or explain every little thing, but perfect the select details you do use to create a memorable or unique world.

The World-Building Checklist

◯ **Add Your Spin**
Write what you know when setting up your world.

◯ **Cue up Some Contrasts**
Add contrasts into your world-building to clue the reader in on how things work, motivate characters, and add elements of depth and tension.

◯ **Set the Rules and Break Them**
Create your rules, establish them on the page, and break them for a good reason.

◯ **Don't Get Trapped**
Keep note or use a series bible to track all details so you don't write yourself into a corner across your book or a series of books.

The Internal Thoughts Checklist

WHILE THERE ARE JUST as many writing tricks as there are ways to tell a story, there are some specific ones that can help make your book special, such as internal thoughts.

If you haven't heard of the concept, it's where you let the reader *inside* a character's head by writing what they're thinking but not saying out loud.

This is a great trick because it gives the reader something extra, like letting them in on a secret.

When to Use Internal Thoughts

To Impart Relatable Thoughts

While we might not always understand the actions of characters because we'd *never* do what they would in the same situation, an internal thought a character might have could strike that familiar chord instead. It's often those thoughts that people think but never say.

Use your character's internal thoughts to reflect...

- Good thoughts.
- Bad thoughts.
- Witty thoughts.
- Innermost truths.

Imagine all the times you've wanted to say something but held your tongue. Could it have made a difference in a situation? Or what if you knew something about someone that they'd never told anyone, would that make you feel closer to them?

Being privy to such thoughts and inner truths would create an instant bond between friends, so why not a reader and a character? That's the power of relatable internal thoughts, so use it.

To Avoid Info-Dumping

Working backstory into your character's history can sometimes come across as info-dumping when you're laying it all out. One way to avoid this is by putting that same history into internal thoughts.

- Have your character internally reminisce about something in their past.
- Have them think back to a situation so they can impart need-to-know info in a more subtle way.

This will get the right info to your readers, without dumping it in paragraph after boring paragraph.

To Ensure Motives Don't Come Out of Nowhere

As the writer penning the story, we know when and why things are happening, but sometimes, we don't put those reasons on the page.

Yep, it happens. We forget to let the reader know something that is perfectly obvious to us.

The good news is that you can fix such an oversight via internal thoughts.

- Include a thought about what your character is thinking and feeling to make their actions more realistic and their motives easier to accept.

If the reader knows *why* your main character had a sudden outburst because they internally debated what was going on around them *first*, it makes things clearer than if they'd just huffed off in the middle of the scene.

When to Dump Internal Thoughts

When There's Entire Paragraphs of Them

Like all good things, internal thoughts can be overdone and be more of an interruption than an interesting writing trick. To avoid such a scenario in your book...

- Don't add too many in a row.

- A good rule of thumb is to add no more than three to a page.

Examples:

Too Many Thoughts:
Jenny stared at the back of Carla's empty seat. **Late as usual. What excuse will she use this time? Did her alarm fail? Did her car not start? Did she have nothing to wear? Clothes too dirty, or not trendy enough. Perhaps she fell down the stairs rushing out the door. Or she lost track of time getting ready. Did her lipstick shade clash with her eyeshadow? Did her mascara run out? Was she at the store spending money she didn't have just so she could fit in with the people who didn't notice Carla was even late today?**

Just Enough:
Jenny stared at the back of Carla's empty seat. **Late as usual. What excuse will she use this time? Failed alarm? Nothing to wear? A last-minute shopping spree for mascara she couldn't afford to fit in with the people who didn't notice Carla was even late today?**

In regards to the first example, while Jenny might think all of these things, and it's a good way to show she's concerned about her friend and what she thinks about Carla trying to keep up with other social circles, there are just too many internal thoughts at once.

By slashing the thoughts in the second example, and sticking to the ones that highlight the info you're trying to establish about Carla's character and Jenny's attitude, you've made great use of internal thoughts, but haven't overwhelmed your reader, who may not make it through an entire paragraph of them.

When It's Padding

During drafting or when you're trying to hit a specific word count, throwing multiple internal thoughts into your paragraphs keeps things moving and contributes to your number of words.

You may have needed it to clarify where your characters were going or what was happening next. It should have been edited out in draft three. It should have definitely been cut during the *final-final-this-time-you-mean-it* draft. Multiple internal thoughts are padding. *You* know it. The reader will know it too.

Look at each internal thought and ask the following:

Could this thought be shown better as...

- Dialogue?
- Action?

If so, do that.

Does this thought...

- Move things forward?
- Show character growth?

If so, keep it.

Does the thought...

- Bring something new to the scene?
- Repeat something obvious?
- Echo an action a character just did?
- States what was just written in the dialogue?

- Drag the scene down?

- Drag the scene on?

- Interrupt the pacing?

- Is still there because *you* love it?

- Asks one/the most important thing at the right time?

- Internally monologues the question and then the exact answer *right after*, robbing the reader of the experience of working out the answer for themselves.

Keep or delete depending on what you're trying to achieve.

And one final tip on internal thoughts is that readers don't need to know *every little thing* that pops into your character's head.

It's an exhausting way to write and read. Use your discretion, double-check with beta readers that you haven't gone internal too much, and then enjoy the depth an excellent trick such as this can bring to your writing.

Related Checklists

The Info-Dumping Checklist
The Character Motivation Checklist

The Internal Thoughts Checklist

◯ **Use to Impart Relatable Thoughts**
Use your character's internal thoughts to reflect good, bad, and witty thoughts, and innermost truths to create a relatable bond with the reader.

◯ **Use to Avoid Info-Dumping**
Use your character's thoughts to internally reminisce and think back to situations to give relevant info and backstory.

◯ **Use to Ensure Motives Don't Come Out of Nowhere**
Let readers know via internal thoughts what the character is thinking, feeling, their motives, and why they're acting like they are.

The Internal Thoughts Checklist

☐ Dump When There's Entire Paragraphs of Them
Don't add too many in a row. A good rule of thumb is to add no more than three internal thoughts to a page.

☐ Dump When It's Padding
Use the listed questions to decide if you should keep or delete.

Could this internal thought be shown better as...
- Dialogue?
- Action?

If so, do that.

Does this thought...
- Move things forward?
- Show character growth?

If so, keep it.

Does the thought...
- Bring something new to the scene?
- Repeat something obvious?
- Echo an action a character just did?
- States what was just written in the dialogue?
- Drag the scene down?
- Drag the scene on?
- Interrupt the pacing?
- Is still there because *you* love it?
- Asks the most important thing at the right time?
- Internally monologues the question and the exact answer right after?

Keep or delete the internal thought, depending on what you're trying to achieve.

The Stakes Checklist

STORY STAKES ARE ONE of those fun writing elements that can make or break the tale you're telling.

With no stakes, a story is in danger of boring the reader. If the stakes are too low, the reader will question why they should care, but if you go to the other extreme and have stakes that are ridiculously high, you could end up with a story so bad it's bound for *Do-Not-Finish* territory.

It's a tricky balance to strike, but one that is worth getting right with the help of this checklist.

Start Small

While it's perfectly fine to start your story with stakes laid bare to get the reader on board, if the first stakes they come across are the biggest, there's just nowhere for the story to go.

- Stakes work best when they start out small.
- Spiral stakes into something bigger.

Build the Stakes

Losing a bet might be a small stake for your main character, but if that bet loss leads to a gambling issue that then leads to a job loss, a relationship loss, and even a loss of life, that small stake builds to the biggest stake of the story and makes things worse for your main character.

- After starting small, it's important to build on the stakes.

That's the beauty of stakes, and that's what will keep readers turning the pages.

Avoid Repeating the Stakes

While you'll need to build the stakes, don't fall into the trap of repeating them.

- Create and keep the tension with different stakes and don't rehash similar stakes.

If you find your main character trapped in the dark more than once, even if it's under different circumstances, you're just repeating stakes to create mini cliffhangers or interesting chapter endings without actually using the stakes to your advantage.

Don't Go Overboard

While your final stake should be big enough to shift your character, circumstances, or outcome, it should never be *so high* that it becomes ridiculous.

- You want the highest stakes to mean something, but if it's too unbelievable, you'll risk screwing up the ending and losing the reader.

One of the fastest ways to lose readers is by ripping away their care factor when the stakes get *so overboard* that your story loses its place in reality. Don't do that.

Personalize the Stakes

Obviously, this depends on the story being told, but if you can...

- Keep the stakes as something that affects the characters.

A bomb killing an office full of random people versus a bomb killing the main character's husband are two *very different* stakes. Both will add interest to your story, but only one will make the reader really care about what is happening.

Add a Condition

When the major stakes are resolved, it's usually down to the main character winning or the main character losing. While both will create a satisfying or a disappointing ending, a win/lose stake resolution can be seen a mile away.

- Resolve the predictable stakes, but add something unpredictable too.

The cop living his career dream and stopping the serial killer from killing the girl is a predictable stake. It will cause the classic good triumphing evil ending that readers expect/want, but in what condition does the cop win? Is he injured so badly during the last battle that he can no longer be a cop?

By adding a condition to the stakes, you'll satisfy the classic side of it, but give something new that the reader will care/think about after finishing the last chapter.

Use Sacrifice Stakes

Stakes that end with a sacrifice are like candy to a sweet tooth, but don't immediately think this means killing off your main character to save the world.

- A sacrifice stake can be small, like the main character giving up their life in the city to move to the country when the cowboy makes them fall in love on that one last trip back home.

- Another option is a side character giving up their share in a business deal so someone else can benefit.

If the story allows it, add a sacrifice stake—big or small—that means something to one or more of your characters. If the sacrifice works for them and the story, it will work for the reader too.

Related Checklists

The Unpredictability Checklist

The Stakes Checklist

○ **Start Small**
Stakes work best when they start small and spiral into something bigger.

○ **Build the Stakes**
Make the stakes bigger to keep readers turning the page.

○ **Avoid Repeating the Stakes**
Keep the tension with different stakes and don't rehash similar stakes.

○ **Don't Go Overboard**
You want the highest stakes to mean something, but if it's too unbelievable, you'll risk losing the reader.

○ **Personalize the Stakes**
Keep the stakes as something that affects the characters personally.

○ **Add a Condition**
Resolve predictable stakes (the good guy winning) but add an unpredictable condition too (the hero being seriously hurt).

○ **Use Sacrifice Stakes**
Add a stake—big or small—where a character/s has to give up something that matters to them.

The Dialogue Tips Checklist

GOOD DIALOGUE IS AN important part of any story, revealing twists, unveiling character, motivations, and giving your cliffhangers the perfect bite. After all, who doesn't love the final line of a scene ending in a suspenseful piece of dialogue.

While it's up to *you* to perfect your dialogue, to ensure it's on track, double-check it with this checklist.

Don't Let It Turn Into a Monologue

When people talk in real life, they get disrupted, either by something or by someone. Rarely do you get the chance to talk on and on and on.

- If your dialogue needs to get a lot of points across, consider how you can work it into the narrative instead.
- Consider turning it into a realistic back-and-forth conversation between characters.
- It might be fun for the villain to reveal the genius of his plan in a well-rehearsed, page-long speech, but it's more fun for the hero—and reader—when that dialogue gets argued with or is cut short by action.

Skip Unnatural Exchanges

While it's hard to inject life experience into a conversation between two characters about taming dragons or the perils of living at the bottom of the sea, any exchange of dialogue should still sound like a conversation two people *would* have.

If your dialogue is...

- Coming off stilted.
- Lacks natural pauses.
- Doesn't have interruptions.
- Doesn't break up with actions beats.
- Doesn't have characters talking over each other/cutting each other off.

It's time to rewrite it for a more natural exchange.

Don't Make It Too Natural

On the flip side, just as you *don't* want to make dialogue too unnatural or formal, you also don't want it to be *too* natural.

- Give conversations crammed with "Umms" and "Ahhs" a miss. A few to signal the speaker going off topic or forgetting what they were saying is fine, but too many is too much.
- Hesitation and fumbles have their place when you're giving the impression of a bumbling or lying character, but simply peppering *every word* that comes out of a character's mouth as a stumble lays it on too thick.

Don't Dismiss Simple Tags

While it's more exciting to write *she exclaimed!* than *she said*, cramming in as many different dialogue tags as you can is more amateurish than artistic.

To make it clear who is speaking, use the tried and true...

- Said

Occasionally, use...

- Whispered.
- Muttered.

- Asked.

- Replied.

- Answered.

Using a different dialogue tag every chance you get creates less impact than if you were to use *one* really great different tag at the perfect point.

Don't Eliminate All Tags

Another option is to avoid making any choices and go without dialogue tags—but there are downsides to it.

- Trying to follow a conversation where there are no dialogue tags is annoying.

- It's confusing for readers.

Keep it to a minimum if you must, but have a tag in there somewhere, especially if the conversation is between more than two characters, it's a long conversation, or there's a lot of action happening in the scene.

Include the Setting

If your characters are failing to acknowledge where they are or what they're doing when talking, you're making it hard for your reader to picture what's going on.

Example:

Dialogue Without a Setting Interaction:
"The reservation was for eight," Jenny said.
"I had to make a stop," Carla replied.

Without knowing the setting, this dialogue comes across as an angry Jenny and a thoughtless Carla. Are they at a restaurant? Are they at home? Are they in the car coming home? Who knows? Now for the same dialogue with a setting added...

Example:

Dialogue with a Setting Interaction:
"The reservation was for eight," Jenny said, **shifting in the cushioned chair as she slipped into the seat across from her.**
"I had to make a stop," Carla replied, **putting the red box down on the wooden table, careful not to disturb the expertly placed ribbon strapped on top.**

Now we can clearly establish they're in a restaurant, Carla is late, and that she comes across as sympathetic and not full of excuses when she places her wrapped gift down on the table.

Use setting interactions with your dialogue—it makes a difference.

Use Different Sames and Quirks

A downside to being the one writer behind a conversation between multiple characters is capturing those differences. You've got to know your characters well to make their dialogue distinct, but even something as subtle as a greeting can set your characters apart.

For example, "Hello" is a common word to use when characters meet, yet if they all said it you'd get something like this...

"Hello."
"Hello."
"Hello."

Boring, huh? Especially with no dialogue tags or action beats to inject personality. Let's try that again with some greeting alternatives...

"Hello."
"Hey."
"Hi!"

Did you read each one of those greetings differently? Did they get more casual or chirpy? Did it sound like it was three different people? The answer is *yes* because each character should have their own way of saying something—even if it's the same thing.

When characters are not saying the same common phrases, readers should be able to tell who is speaking simply by looking at the rest of the character's dialogue.

- Giving each character a dialogue quirk specific to them will go a long way to making sure that none of your characters sound the same.

That doesn't mean giving everyone a different accent (unless your plot calls for it) but something more subtle, such as a specific character being the only one in the story to use the word *awesome*.

Avoid Small Talk

Just like in life, small talk has a time and a place. Usually, that time and place doesn't belong in your book.

- Sometimes, small talk may show that something is awkward or boring, but unless it moves the plot forward, don't waste your precious dialogue.

No one needs to know Carla says "The sky is pretty blue today" when she meets Jenny in the park with a mysterious package. Save the dialogue for the interesting stuff, i.e. "Keep the package sealed. Don't open it here in the park."

Expel Exposition

This is another time and place instance. Using your dialogue to rattle off your main character's theory about who committed a spate of murders twenty years ago can work *if* the dialogue is a compelling back and forth between your main character and the sheriff who botched the original investigation but refuses to admit it. If it's not, then your dialogue is just full of boring exposition.

Leave the exposition out of the dialogue...

- If it's not edge-of-your-seat, what-will-they-say-next? level stuff.
- If it's coming across as two characters throwing facts at each other.

You can get the same info across using your show, don't tell skills instead.

Balance Name Drops

I'm a fence sitter on this. Some writers say mentioning names in dialogue is a waste of good dialogue and redundant, but I've used it in conversations that needed dramatic tension or in action scenes, and I think it works just fine.

If you're happy with using names to make a point, do it. Just don't overuse them, like so...

"How are you today, **Carla**?"
"I'm fine, **Jenny**. And you?"
"Just great thanks, **Carla**."
"That's super, **Jenny**."

Read It Out Loud

Once you've mastered these dialogue tips, don't forget to give your dialogue an out loud read. It will give you the chance to...

- Assess if it sounds natural.

- Identify where any pauses might need to be.

- Decide if it's too wordy.

- Flag anything awkward sounding.

If your dialogue doesn't sound like a conversation you'd overhear at a café, rewrite it. And if you know the best way to look as if you're *not* listening to public conversations—when in fact you totally are—let me know. I'm asking for a friend...

Related Checklists

The Settings Checklist
The Distinct Characters Checklist
The Dialogue Checklist

The Dialogue Tip Checklist

☐ **Don't Let It Turn Into a Monologue**
It's fun for the villain to reveal plans in page-long speeches, but it's more fun for the reader when that dialogue gets argued with or is cut short by action.

☐ **Skip Unnatural Exchanges**
Dialogue exchanges should sound like a conversation two people would have. Include natural pauses, interruptions, characters talking over/cutting each other off, and action beats.

☐ **Don't Make It Too Natural**
Hesitation and fumbles have their place when you're giving the impression of a bumbling or lying character, but peppering every word as a stumble lays it on too thick.

☐ **Don't Dismiss Simple Tags**
Cramming in lots of different dialogue tags is more amateurish than artistic and creates less impact than if you used a great tag at the perfect point.

☐ **Don't Eliminate All Tags**
Trying to follow a conversation where there are no dialogue tags is confusing. Keep them to a minimum over elimination.

☐ **Include the Setting**
Use setting interactions with your dialogue so the reader can picture where or when the characters are.

The Dialogue Tip Checklist

◯ **Use Different Sames and Quirks**
Each character should have their own way of saying something—even if it's the same thing. Giving characters their own dialogue quirk, such as one being the only person who says "Awesome," helps.

◯ **Avoid Small Talk**
Unless it moves the plot forward, don't waste your precious dialogue on small talk.

◯ **Expel Exposition**
Leave the exposition out of the dialogue if it's not edge-of-your-seat stuff or if it's coming across as two characters throwing facts at each other.

◯ **Balance Name Drops**
Some writers think mentioning names in dialogue is a waste of good dialogue, but it can add dramatic tension. Just make sure you're not over-using them.

◯ **Read It Out Loud**
Give your dialogue an out loud read to assess naturalness, identify needed pauses, test if it's wordy, and to flag anything awkward.

Outlining

In this section, you'll find a checklist that will help you outline your manuscript *after* you have written the first draft. You can also go back to this outline and use it again anytime you have completed a draft to help you plan where to take the story next.

The Reverse Outline Checklist

If you're a writer who is a planner, one of the first things you'll do when starting a new manuscript is create an outline. If you're a pantser (raises hand), you'll shun outlining in favor of writing by the seat of your pants—aka—*not* knowing what you're doing until you've done it.

You might have the incident that kicks the story off or a vague idea about small-town secrets without actually knowing what that secret is yet, but you're hopeful you'll get the details as you write—provided you've made enough offerings of chocolate to satisfy your muse.

Writing without a plan might be the only way some pantsers can work, but eventually, you'll need something to make sense of all those chapters, and that's when reverse outlining can help.

How to Reverse Outline

Reverse outlining is where you sit down *after* you've written your first draft and outline your book. It helps you see the whole story, breaks down the incidents, highlights character motivations, and allows you to make a game plan for the second draft.

This is what I do, but feel free to chop it, change it, and add your own process to the basics.

- Get yourself a notebook or create a new document in your fave writing program.

I like to reverse outline in a notebook so that I can easily look at the notes while working on the next draft from my computer screen. This also has the bonus of creating some fun when you try to understand what you've handwritten. If that's a problem you *don't* want, create your outline in a digital file.

Start at Chapter One and Break Down What Happens

Your notes don't need to be detailed, just a few words or bullet points on:

- What happens.
- Who is in the chapter.
- What incidents occur and why.

Highlight the Highlights

Once you have every chapter broken down, go back over your notes and highlight the important parts:

- Reveals.
- Plots twists.
- Moments of despair.
- Moments of triumph.
- Anything of significance.

Make a List of What Needs to Be Added/Done

Thanks to your highlights, you should now be able to see how many plot holes need to be filled, if you have too many characters, where you need an event to prop up the sagging middle chapters, and if your villain reveal will work better three chapters earlier.

With all of that established:

- Make a new list of what you need to do to fix the issues.

Some writers like to tackle the big issues first, then work through the smaller problems on a chapter by chapter level, or you might like to do the easy fixes first.

You may also have other steps that you want to include, but for me, keeping the reverse outline as simple as possible means that I can get to the second draft sooner. It also keeps rewriting and editing at a comfortable level instead of making it too overwhelming.

After the next draft has been written, you might outline again if it feels like the plot is missing something. More often than not, though, one reverse outline is enough to get a grasp on what's written and to work out where to go from there.

Related Checklists

The What to Establish in a Scene Checklist
The Something Is Missing Checklist

 # The Reverse Outline Checklist

⭕ Break Down What Happens

Start at chapter one and bullet point and write basic notes about:

- What happens.
- Who is in the chapter.
- What incidents occur and why.

⭕ Highlight the Highlights

Highlight the important parts:

- Reveals.
- Plots twists.
- Moments of despair.
- Moments of triumph.
- Anything of significance.

⭕ Make a List of What Needs to be Added/Done

Based on the above, work through this list when you plan/write your next draft.

Drafts

To help you at the start of the writing process, and the end, here are two drafting checklists that will teach you how to create, fatten, and trim down your manuscript, as well as provide you with ways to check the finer details to get your work as close to the final draft as possible.

The Three Draft Checklist

WHIPPING A BOOK INTO shape takes time and effort. Growing something from an idea into a fully fledged story with characters and events will require stamina and lots of rewriting.

One way to make that process easier is to implement a great drafting system, one where the first three drafts will provide you with what you'll need to create the foundation for your story.

Start with the Bones

Your **first draft** just needs to get the story out. To do that...

- Write the bare minimum, whatever words you need to get the pages filled and the plot moving in a forward direction.

- Even basic sentences such as, "He walked from one room to the next," are enough at this stage to start the bones of what will be your book.

Don't worry about the word count, how long it will take to write, if anyone will want to read it, how it's going to end, or what you're going to say. *Just write the damn thing*.

When you move on to the second draft, you'll cut up, chop, and change your first draft so much, there will be sections of your book *only you* will ever see. Enjoy having that special connection with your work.

Fatten It Up

The **second draft** needs to take those bones and add some substance.

- Fill in your detail and thicken your sentences.

- Add to the plot.

- Establish your characters and their traits.

- Take your basic sentences and expand on them.

Example:

He walked from one room to the next.

Becomes...

He took a step, one foot, and then another, in front of each other, until he had cleared the big, wide doorway and crossed over the emptiness of the abandoned hallway to complete his arrival in the next room.

There's more detail, interest, and atmosphere added to the sentence, which is what a great second draft should do.

After you've expanded everything, it's time for another draft.

Get Lean

The **third draft** is all about trimming the excess. Overindulging in the words was fun, but now it's time to cut the fat.

- Get rid of anything that doesn't advance the plot, add to the characters and enhance the story.

- Remove excess words that clutter your sentences.

- Get rid of storylines that go nowhere.

- Eliminate excessive characters.

Example:

That fattened sentence goes from...

He took a step, one foot, and then another, in front of each other, until he had cleared the big, wide doorway and crossed over the emptiness of the abandoned hallway to complete his arrival in the next room.

To this:

He took a step, one foot in front of the other, until he had cleared the wide doorway and crossed the abandoned hall to arrive in the next room.

The sentence is now tighter and leaner. The needless words are cut, but the interest and enough detail remain.

This is the purpose of the third draft. It will allow you to see the overall story with the added details, but it isn't weighed down by the unnecessary.

While drafting is as a personal process, and it's up to you to decide how many drafts it'll take to complete your story, you should find it easier to work on your subsequent drafts after using three drafts to firstly establish, fatten, and then trim your overall story.

Related Checklists

The Under Writing Checklist
The Over Writing Checklist
The Early Draft Cuts Checklist
The Final Draft Checklist

The Three Draft Checklist

○ Start with the Bones
Use your first draft to just write. Use whatever basic words and details will get the pages filled and the plot moving.

○ Fatten It Up
Use the second draft to add details to sentences, deepen your plot, and establish your characters.

○ Get Lean
For the third draft, cut the excess of words, storylines that don't advance the plot, and characters that don't work.

The Final Draft Checklist

You know that meme where writers name their files *Final Draft, Final Draft 2, Final Draft 3, Really Final Draft, Really, Really Final Draft, Seriously Final Draft*, etc.

Past-You probably thought by now you'd be doing that, but Present-You just spent eight months rewriting your latest draft and knows Future-You still has at least one more to go.

Did you plan to rewrite for eight months? *No.* Did you want it to take eight months? *Double no.* Do you want the next draft to take that long? *Hell no.*

To get to the real "Final Draft" it's time to get a little organized, a little crafty, a little planner-like, and tackle this next draft efficiently and quickly, with the help of this checklist.

Check the Outline

By the time you're a few drafts deep, you should know your story well. Still, when you've been tinkering with sentences, cutting darlings, and adding to your word count, it's possible you've changed something or added a plot hole and not noticed.

- Take your outline (or write one if needed) and make sure your current draft follows it.

It's also a good refresher of the story and it'll help you plan your synopsis, which you know is coming because you're almost at the final draft (probably).

Check the Chapter Lengths

With your plot set, check your foundations. Do you have enough chapters? Do you have too many? Are they the length you want them to be?

- Check the length of your chapters.
- Split up chapters that are too long.
- Renumber everything.
- Make sure the chapters are the right length.
- Ensure the chapters are in the right order for the story.

Check the Openings and Endings

Once your chapters are sorted...

- Read the first sentence.
- Read the last sentence.

Reading **the first** chapter sentence is to double-check that you haven't used an opening line you've used before. Trust me, it happens. When you're at chapter thirty and you wrote chapter fifteen six months ago, you will *not* remember that you used nearly the same phrasing. You also want to make sure the first sentence hooks the reader.

For **the last** chapter sentence, see that it ends with a bit of drama, such as a cliffhanger, a line of dialogue with some sting in it, or a shocking reveal. Whatever will get the reader to turn the page, and again, an ending that *isn't* a repeat/remixed version of another chapter.

Check for Notes

I don't know about you, but I have a habit of putting notes in brackets where I need to make the changes and highlighting them in yellow. I also have a habit of forgetting I've done this. That means one final draft checklist item is to look for such notes, make any changes still outstanding, and delete out the highlighted part.

- Delete any notes you've made for yourself within the sentences or at the ends of paragraphs, chapters, etc.

- Remove any highlighting, underlining, bolding, or other formatting that isn't supposed to be part of the book.

Check the Checklists

Okay, now that you've got your plot set, chapters numbered, the openings, endings, and lengths right, and removed your notes, it's time for the hard work to begin.

It's checklist time. This is when you'll spend your days getting cozy with your *find/search* function and working through your checklists for words that can be deleted or rewritten for better prose.

This is the task that will take the most time to complete and where you'll learn that you use the word "that" *way too much*.

Use the following checklists from this book, and pair it with some chocolate to fuel yourself through.

- *The Delete Checklist* will help make your sentences less wordy.

- *The Weak Word Checklist* removes words that weaken your sentences.

- *The Active Checklist* keeps your prose active.

Check with a Spelling Program

After you've used the checklists to nitpick your sentences, run the manuscript through a spelling/grammar program and check for...

- Typos.

- Double words (I also have a habit of typing things like "the the" and not noticing).

- Readability.
- Any relevant reports the program offers.

These types of editing programs are helpful in terms of another set of eyes, but don't rely on them completely or trust that every suggestion they give is correct. Use your own instincts too.

Check with Your Ears

By now, you're sick of reading your words. You know this manuscript forward, backward, and sideways and can no longer trust your eyes to read what's on the page versus what your brain *thinks* is on the page.

When you get to this point, it's time to switch to either reading out loud yourself or having a program read the words to you.

- Use a text-to-speech app.
- Load the manuscript in Word and use their speak option.
- Use whatever program you have that allows text to speech, or a read-aloud function.

During this run-through, you should find awkward sentences, typos (because they're always there, lurking in your perfectly crafted sentences), and mistakes your eyes will gloss over at this point.

Check with Someone Else

The final check is having someone else read your manuscript.

- Rope in a friend.
- Ask a family member.
- Beta read swap with a fellow author.

Preferably use someone who hasn't read the manuscript before as they will have the freshest eyes and should be able to pick up on anything that's been missed.

Once they've given their feedback and you implement any changes, fix typos they found etc, that's it.

You've now checked the outline, chapters, editing notes, checklists, and used your ears, writing programs, and betas. All of that should be *more than enough* to officially name the file your *Final Draft* and mean it.

After that you're allowed one *Final Draft 2*, maybe a *Final Draft 3*, but then a *Seriously Final Draft* should be where you draw the line.

Okay, maybe a *Seriously, Seriously, Seriously Final Draft* after that—but that's it!

Seriously.

Related Checklists

The Three Draft Checklist
The Reverse Outline Checklist
The Book Openings Checklist
The Chapter Endings Checklist
The Fresh Eyes Typo Hunting Checklist

✓ The Final Draft Checklist

○ **Check the Outline**
Take your outline (or write one if needed) and make sure your current draft follows it.

○ **Check the Chapter Lengths**
Do you have enough chapters? Do you have too many?

- Check the length of your chapters.
- Split up chapters that are too long.
- Renumber everything.
- Make sure the chapters are the right length.
- Ensure the chapters are in the right order for the story.

○ **Check the Openings and Endings**

- Read the first sentence of every chapter to make sure it's not the same phrasing as another.
- Read the last sentence of every chapter to make the same check and to see that it ends in a way that will encourage the reader to turn the page.

○ **Check for Notes**
Take out any notes you've left for yourself, highlighted words/sentences, or formatting that shouldn't be there.

✓ The Final Draft Checklist

◯ **Check the Checklists**
Get cozy with your *find/search* function and work through these checklists:

- The Delete Checklist.
- The Weak Word Checklist.
- The Active Word Checklist.

◯ **Check with a Spelling Program**
Run the manuscript through a spelling/grammar program to find typos, double words, and grammatical errors.

◯ **Check with Your Ears**
Read your book out loud or have a text-to-speech app read it to you to find awkward sentences and typos.

◯ **Check with Someone Else**
Have someone else read your manuscript and let you know of any errors.

Word Count

The checklists in this section will provide you with all you'll need to add words if you under write, slash words if you over write, and how to reduce a big word count if your final manuscript is way too long.

The Reduce a Big Word Count Checklist

As a writer penning a book, there will be times when *no matter* how tight you've made your storyline, or how close you've stuck to your plan, you've gone over your word count.

And not by a little. *By a lot*. So much so that you're 20,000 extra words deep and haven't even started the edits that give detailed life to your book world.

With that amount of excessive words you'll need to make drastic cuts, and if you have no clue how to do that, this checklist will help.

Cut One Event

When your draft is complete and you know how much needs to be cut, *really* look at what has to be included in your overall story.

If you cast a critical eye, I'm sure you'll find at least *one event* that could lift out.

- Perhaps this event snuck in during the drafting stage when you didn't know where the story was heading and you've kept it in.
- Maybe it's an idea that doesn't work as well as it should, but you love it so much, you've convinced yourself it needs to stay.

It's the ultimate kill-your-darlings test. If you can't make such a cut, ask someone trusted who isn't as attached to the story to advise which element can be removed without losing what's important.

You'll likely find cutting this event makes the story better. Just remember to move any relevant reveals or info into the chapters you're keeping.

Cut the Boring Bits

You might think nothing in your book is boring and that every word creates a sentence that's needed, but that could be why your word count is so high. It's time to be ruthless and cut the boring bits.

- The paragraphs even *you* gloss over when you're reading your work.
- The scene that doesn't do its job of moving the story along.
- The scene that doesn't deepen your characters.

No matter if it has the best sunset description you've ever committed to paper, or invokes one of your favorite memories, if it even hints at an eyes-glaze-over vibe, give it the flick.

Cut Weak Words

We all have certain words that we use too much. What we also don't realize about these words is how much of a difference cutting them makes. This will not only benefit your word count but also add clarity to your sentences.

Although clearing your manuscript of weak words takes time and is mind-numbingly tedious, it's going to eliminate thousands of words and is well worth doing.

- Use the instructions from *The Weak Word Checklist* to get yourself acquainted with the process.
- Make your *find/search* function your best excess word slaying tool.

Cut the Over-Explaining

Hands up if you need to make things clear to yourself as you're writing. That's me too. I'm also so excellent at stage directing that a character doesn't move without *every detail* described exactly.

You might need those things to get the story on the page, to understand what you're doing and where you're going as you pants your way through each chapter, but once the story is set, it's time to cut the over-explaining.

- Look at your sentences and adopt the mantra: simple, tight, and precise.

Examples:

Excess Word Count: She crouched down and then reached her hand toward the ball.
Simple, Tight, Precise (Slight Rewrite): She crouched and reached for the ball.

Excess Word Count: She started to walk up the stairs.
Simple, Tight, Precise (Slight Rewrite): She walked up the stairs.

See the difference cutting the over-explaining words can make. The reader still knows what's happening, the sentence is more active, and you've cut words.

Cut Repetitive Mentions

This is another writing habit that contributes to big word counts. It usually crops up when you've been writing an manuscript over a long period (months or years) and have forgotten that you've already mentioned the main character's habit of collecting sea shells in chapter three, have brought it again in chapter fifteen, and then while working on chapter thirty-five for good measure.

- Unless something is *extremely* important to the plot and needs to be mentioned more than once for emphasis or closer to a payoff so the reader connects the dots, make sure you haven't mentioned the same thing too many times.

- Key info in the right place is more important.

Aim for that goal and get rid of any repetitive mentions.

With the art of writing, no words are wasted. Crafting them makes you a better writer, as does knowing when and where to delete them.

Don't be afraid of cutting to reduce a big word count. It's usually exactly what your story needs and is a great writing skill that will serve you well for many manuscripts to come.

Related Checklists

The Under Writing Checklist
The Over Writing Checklist
The Final Draft Checklist
The Delete Checklist

✓ The Reduce a Big Word Count Checklist

◯ **Cut One Event**
Cast a critical eye and find one event that could lift out.

◯ **Cut the Boring Bits**
If it even hints at an eyes-glaze-over vibe, give it the flick.

◯ **Cut Weak Words**
Use the instructions from The Weak Word Checklist to get yourself acquainted with the process of cutting words that add nothing to your sentences.

◯ **Cut the Over-Explaining**
Look at your sentences and adopt the mantra: simple, tight, and precise.

◯ **Cut Repetitive Mentions**
Unless something is extremely important to the plot and needs to be mentioned more than once for emphasis or close to a payoff, make sure you haven't mentioned the same thing too many times.

The Under Writing Checklist

IF YOU'RE A CHRONIC over writer, under writing might not be a problem for you, but it's not just about finding it hard to write enough words. Under writing also involves leaving out details that can rob your characters of depth and your story of important info.

If that's something you've done when penning your manuscripts, or you'd like to know more about under writing problems and fixes, this checklist is for you.

You Have a Low Word Count

This is probably the first thing most people think about when they hear the term underwriting.

Not reaching a certain word count, or not being able to write enough to complete a scene, is the most common form of underwriting, but there are ways to fix the problem. All it takes is practice and new habits.

- Set yourself a word count.
- Break it down into chapters and then scenes.

Just like a short story might be capped at a certain length for submission/publishing purposes, so will a book. Industry standards are a Google search away and will give you something to aim for.

Knowing a scene needs to be 1,200 words could be all the push you need to raise your low word count.

For an underwriter, that'll be overwhelming at first, but the more you get used to writing a certain amount of words, the easier it will get.

You're Missing Internal Thoughts/Feelings

If you've ever connected with a character in a book, it's because you relate to them and/or have gotten to know them. One way writers achieve this is by using internal thoughts, aka, putting the reader inside the head of the character.

If your story doesn't include internal thoughts, or enough of them, it's contributing to your underwriting.

The same goes for feelings. What are your characters feeling when things happen to them? Make sure you include it.

- Add/increase the level of internal character thoughts.

- Let the reader know how characters feel about things, especially the big stuff.

You can do this with a monologue of thoughts or even via showing. Everyone knows to show emotion rather than tell it, i.e. "She threw the chair" versus "She was angry," but don't forget to add the thoughts behind the anger from your characters. It'll help your under writing and add depth.

There's Plenty of Scenes but No Sequels

As a reader and a writer, I prefer books that get straight into things and keep it moving to the last page. I don't need chapters wasted on characters sitting around doing nothing. However, just sticking to the exciting parts can contribute to underwriting.

If it's all go-go action, not only will you fail to write enough, you'll also miss out on creating a well-rounded story and characters.

The same applies to reactions. For everything that happens to your character, there should be a reaction. Don't just drop a bombshell and then move on without showing the consequences.

- Any action/event scenes need to be balanced with a sequel where the character and reader process what has happened.

It doesn't need to be a 3,000-word chapter on their feelings, but if there's a scene where your main character is hurt and they then go about their business like nothing happened, it's not only unrealistic, it's bad underwriting.

Include immediate reactions to the events in your book and watch it drive your word count up.

The Main Plot Doesn't Stretch Far Enough

Well, you've done it! A brilliant idea popped into your head. You executed the premise perfectly; the characters wrote themselves, and the plot flows perfectly from the first page to last—all 50 of them.

As good as your main plot is, if it doesn't stretch far enough, you won't just be under writing a book, you'll be creating a short story instead.

- Explore a subplot.
- Brainstorm new ideas/what-ifs.
- Think about characters that might be missing.
- Ponder events that could happen, like if your characters did something else between robbing the bank and then getting caught.

These ideas could help round your book out in ways you hadn't expected, which will only make the main plot even stronger and help you craft a story that is far from underwritten.

You've Skipped Decision Processes

Sometimes when we're eager to get from one event to another, we forget to add those little in-between moments that, although small, make a big difference to your story.

One such example is decision processes. When you omit a decision process from a character, not only is it another form of underwriting, it's also confusing for the reader.

For example, a character being adamant they *don't* want to go to a party with their friends and then turning up at said party is jarring. But, if you've established that they've changed their mind and put that decision on the page, it won't be so out of the blue.

- Check that all character acts are backed up by decisions the reader is told about.

- Make sure whatever decision the character makes can be surmised by what else you've put on the page.

Sometimes this missing info isn't there because you've accidentally edited it out or it's in your head but not on the page. We've all been there.

You Have Thin Set Ups and Resolutions

This kind of under writing pops up when you rush the set up with poorly detailed setting descriptions, or by not putting enough into your world-building.

When your book's world is thinly set up, it makes it hard for the reader to get into the story. It also robs your book of vivid, image-inducing paragraphs that will give you the word count that an under writer dreams of.

Another place where a lack of words can be increased is in your resolutions. You might have nailed the main character getting their objective, but if it happened so quickly that it's over in a page, it does little else than create an unsatisfying read.

- Ensure your settings are well-described.

- Include vivid descriptions so readers get the full picture.

- Don't rush the resolutions to big events.

So, there you have some under writing problems and fixes. While this checklist doesn't cover everything, hopefully it provides enough advice to inspire more words and depth for your manuscript if under writing is a problem for you.

Related Checklists

The Reduce a Big Word Count Checklist
The Over Writing Checklist

The Under Writing Checklist

○ **You Have a Low Word Count**
Set a word count goal and break it down into chapters and then scenes so you know where to add more words.

○ **You're Missing Internal Thoughts/Feelings**
If your story doesn't include internal thoughts/feelings, or enough of them, add more, and use as much show instead of tell as you can.

○ **There's Plenty of Scenes but No Sequels**
Any big action/event scene needs to be balanced with a sequel where the character and reader process what has happened.

○ **The Main Plot Doesn't Stretch Far Enough**
Explore a subplot, brainstorm new ideas/what-ifs, and think about extra events your characters can do in between the main ones.

○ **You've Skipped Decision Processes**
Check that your character acts are backed up by decisions the reader is told about or can surmise by what else is on the page.

○ **You Have Thin Set Ups and Resolutions**
Ensure your settings are well-described, include vivid descriptions, and don't rush the resolutions to big events.

The Over Writing Checklist

THERE ARE A FEW writer-world problems you can have. The muse taking an extended break, losing a month's worth of progress to backup failure, or realizing the unique book idea you've been working on for five years was just published by someone else.

Then there's writer-problems you can fix, such as curbing the need to over write. For that, you'll need this checklist.

Cut Unnecessary Words

If you haven't searched your manuscript for the word *That* have you really edited?

"That" is the queen of unnecessary words, and in most cases can be cut without losing the meaning of the sentence. "Always" is another word that sneaks in and likes to fatten your sentences. In fact, there are plenty of little words that worked fine as you were stringing them together, but can now be removed to make the most of your sentences instead.

- Use *The Delete Checklist* to find as many as you can.

When you trim away those unnecessary words and see your paragraphs are still perfectly telling your story in a clear, concise manner, you'll understand how over writing can muddy your work.

Kill/Combine Characters

Over writing isn't just about extra words on every page, it's also about what happens on the page and who it happens to.

In those early first drafts, when you're telling yourself the story and getting everything that comes into your head on the page, it's easy to miss that sometimes those ideas don't work.

It's even easier to miss that sometimes a character doesn't work. You've put them through so much on your journey to the last draft, deleting them entirely would be soul-destroying. But do you know what a character who does nothing but take up sentences destroys? A good story.

- Study each character, examine what they bring to the story, and decide if they're worth keeping.

- If a character lifts right out, changing nothing major, cut them.

- If you can take their purpose and give it to another character where it ups the stakes, do that.

Sometimes it's necessary to cut a character and sometimes it's necessary to combine two minor characters into one to eliminate your over writing.

Tighten Each Sentence

A step further than deleting unnecessary words is tightening each sentence.

- Take a hard look at every sentence in your manuscript and work out if you can rewrite it with fewer words.

Examples:

Overwritten: Jenny squinted at the bright, sparkly silver sequins on Carla's short, tight dress.

Tightened: Jenny squinted at the silver sequins on Carla's minidress.

We still get the impression of how Carla's dress looks—just as a tighter sentence.

Fill In the Right Details

Nailing description is an art-form. Knowing what to describe so the reader can picture your setting or what a character looks like takes skill. When you're learning this skill, it's so easy to put down every descriptive word out there.

Purple-prosing your descriptions is over writing 101, and the key to cutting down on it is learning to fill in the right details.

Sure, a reader might need to know what kind of café the main character is meeting her love interest in. Set the scene with coffee aromas, colorful tabletops, and the delicious cake treats she buys for her. Just *don't* over write it.

Describing the coffee scent down to the bean and where it was manufactured, the specific hue of each quirky table and how it matches the cupcake icing described in such detail every reader could be a contestant on *Cupcake Wars* is *not* the way to go.

- Perfect crafting your descriptions with the right imagery in as few words as you can.

There's adding details that set a scene, and there's wasting words and the reader's time.

Take Out Repetitive Ideas

Readers read at different paces. While one might devour a book in a whole day, another will read the first two chapters, put the book down for six months, then read chapter three to nine before finally finishing the book after another extended break. For these types of readers, it's a good idea to include a recap of events.

- Add something as simple as another character reminding the main character (and the reader) in the middle of the book about certain things that happened at the start through an off-the-cuff remark.

- Look for every instance of specific/certain info and decide where it's best placed in your book, then delete every other mention.

Doing this repeats something that has already happened, but it's not overwriting. Where it veers into repetitive over writing is when you express the same idea over and over again. For example, if your main character is using the loss of a loved one as motivation, mention it once, maybe twice. If you mention it every single time they do anything at all, it's words that can be slashed.

Watch Your Body Movements

Check to see how many times your characters...

- Nod.
- Reach their hands out.
- Look up.
- Look right.
- Look sideways.
- Any other combination of body movements.

You may think you're being specific. You may think typing out every single movement is fine, but it's overwriting.

Make the character movements clear and concise, omit the movements that aren't necessary, and watch your word count shrink.

Related Checklists

The Reduce a Big Word Count Checklist
The Under Writing Checklist

The Over Writing Checklist

◯ **Cut Unnecessary Words**
Trim unnecessary words to tell your story in a clear, concise manner. Use The Delete Checklist to help you.

◯ **Kill/Combine Characters**
If they don't work, can be omitted without changing the story, or two minor characters can be combined into one, do it.

◯ **Tighten Each Sentence**
Take a hard look at every sentence in your manuscript and work out if you can rewrite it with fewer words.

◯ **Fill In the Right Details**
Learn to fill in the right details with the right imagery in as few words as you can.

◯ **Take Out Repetitive Ideas**
Look for every instance of specific/certain info and decide where it's best placed in your book, then delete every other mention.

◯ **Watch Your Body Movements**
Check to see how many times your characters nod, reach their hands out, or any other combination of useless body movements, and delete the excess.

Openings

The following checklist will help you nail the opening of your book, and once you know the tricks, can improve the opening of your chapters or scenes.

The Book Openings Checklist

IF YOU'VE ENTRENCHED YOURSELF in the writing world, you've no doubt heard what *doesn't* make for a good book opening.

These tips range from ditching prologues to the ultimate pressure inducing advice: the opening sentence/paragraph/page *must* automatically engage the reader or they won't read on.

While this advice is enough to make you consider taking up a different career, ultimately, you should open your book with whatever is right for the story.

Stellar Starts

Another classic piece of writing advice is to start where the story starts. If hearing/reading that advice makes you roll your eyes because, of course, you've started where the story starts, *are you sure?*

Let's say you're writing a heist caper and you've opened your first chapter with the would-be robbers in a van at dusk staking out the bank they're about to rob. With this type of opening, you're introducing the main character and any secondary characters, and you're establishing a setting and time. The dialogue between characters even spells out the plan as they run through their checks. You're doing everything right for an opening chapter. But, what if instead of starting your book at the planning of the heist, you start it right in the middle?

The same characters are introduced. You're still establishing the setting as a bank, but you've put the reader right in the action. They're there with the characters as they're pulling off the heist, perhaps right when everything is going to plan or going wrong.

Anything you wanted to introduce with the slower van opening, such as a connection between the main character and their accomplice or the reason for the heist can all be given after the start, dripped in as the story moves along to create an air of mystery with unanswered questions.

- Start where the meat of the story starts.

- Establish the tone of your book. If it's horror, and you've opened with *anything but* something creepy, it'll only lead to confusion for your readers when chapter two kicks off with a demon hunt.

Use the right opening to pave the way for everything else.

Orientate the Reader

Unless you're really going for something out there, the reader should...

- Know *where* the book is taking place.

- *When* the book is taking place.

It could be on an alien planet 1,000 years in the future, or back in the '90s on the first day of high school. Just let the reader know.

Introduce the Main Character

Where and when works better when readers also know with *whom*. If you can, make the first character your reader meets your main character or the set of characters that you want them to like.

- Introduce the main character or the lead characters who your readers will spend most of the story with. Establish that rapport ASAP.

- If that doesn't work for the first chapter, introduce the main character as soon as possible.

- Do something that will endear them to the reader so they're sympathetic/relatable.

The earlier you do this in your book, the better. You want the reader and your main character to form a connection that will take them from the first page to the last.

Exceptions are, of course, prologues, instances where you need to start with the killer to set up a murder, or opening your story with a flashback or flashforward.

Go for a Basic Backstory

Another of those don'ts you might have heard about is weighing your opening down with backstory. Trouble is, sometimes the only way to get the reader to relate to your main character, or know where or when they are, is through backstory.

- Limit it to the very basics.

Sticking to a throwaway line about the main character being an orphan, or the alien planet's air being easier to move through than the training simulations they used back home, is all you need to put some backstory in an opening that can be expanded on later.

Get Into the Action

This is not a suggestion to start your book with an explosion, but at a place where *something* is happening.

- Open your book with a catalyst that changes things. It could be the smash of a coffee mug as the final bingo number is called out at the senior center game night, or the thud of a murderer pushing a body into a freshly dug grave.

- *Don't* start with your main character getting out of bed, making breakfast, eating breakfast, getting dressed, and going off to start their day.

They could be heading out the door to a morning where the bank they work in gets robbed, or a minor car accident on the commute introduces them to the love of their life. Start at the robbery or the car-crunching fender bender. Get into the action ASAP.

Set Expectations

If your book opens with a murder, the reader will expect a thriller or a mystery. If that murder is never mentioned again, and chapter two is all about a happy couple planning a wedding, they'll wonder if there was a printing error.

- Use the start of your book to set the expectations for what to come.

- Create a tone and voice that will lay the right foundation. If your book is supposed to be humorous, start with a sarcastic sentence to establish it.

World Peek

There's nothing worse than an opening where the reader has *no idea* of the setting. It's confusing, and when readers are confused, they get frustrated. Don't do that to yourself, especially in an opening chapter when you have such little time to get things moving.

- Establish just a peek at your book world as the first chapter is *not* the time or place to info-dump every little thing about how your book world functions.

- Choose simple key elements to highlight what will place your characters and readers in your world and leave everything else for the following chapters.

- Remember that you have an entire book to world-build.

If you're working in the known, modern world, it's easy to quickly establish this for your readers. Your main character could be using their smartphone waiting for a Rideshare. Just those two simple things will let the reader know where and when they are just as easily as a description of your main character in full armor galloping across a field on a horse preparing to draw their sword means they *aren't* in modern times.

If you can work these suggestions into your openings, the reader will want to know how things pan out and will have numerous reasons to keep reading once they've cracked open your book.

Related Checklists

The Chapter Endings Checklist
The Book Endings Checklist

The Book Openings Checklist

◯ **Stellar Starts**
Start at the meat of the story and establish the tone of your book. If it's horror, and you've opened with anything but, it'll only lead to confusion when chapter 2 kicks off with a demon hunt.

◯ **Orientate the Reader**
The reader should know where the book is taking place and when.

◯ **Introduce the Main Character**
Try to make the first character readers meet your main character, or the set of characters you want them to like, and do something that will endear them to the reader.

◯ **Go for a Basic Backstory**
Limit it to the very basics, such as a throwaway line about the main character being an orphan that can be expanded on later.

◯ **Get Into the Action**
Start at a place where something is happening—a catalyst that changes things, not just the boring main character gets out of bed and starts getting ready for their day stereotype.

◯ **Set Expectations**
Use your book opening to set the expectations for what's to come with the right events, tone, and voice.

◯ **World Peek**
Establish just a peek at your book world as the first chapter is *not* the time or place to info-dump everything about how your book world functions.

Endings

To make the most of the ending for both your book and every chapter in it, you'll find two checklists here that will help.

The Chapter Endings Checklist

EVERY WRITER KNOWS THEY need to nail the ending of their book to give readers the satisfaction they deserve, but what about the endings of your chapters?

If you've put little thought into how you're finishing your chapters, then you're missing out on a key component of what makes a good book great. After all, what kind of writer doesn't want readers to say they couldn't put their novel down? To give your tome such a chance, run through this checklist.

Create Conflict

Conflict is at the heart of every story. Even emotionally uplifting stories need a little to hold the reader's interest, and when is the best time to add some? The end of a chapter, of course!

- Add conflict to the last paragraph of the last page of a feel-good chapter.

Conflict right then will grab the reader, and they'll want to read on to see where things go, so end your chapter with something that disrupts the status quo and make the job easy for them.

Elicit New Emotions

Obviously, an emotional chapter ending depends on where your story is heading, but if you can start a chapter with your main character feeling one way and then end it with a completely different emotion, chances are readers will want to know how this new turmoil will play out.

- Make it so that a main character who is feeling on top of the world at the start of the chapter, has everything flipped on them at the end.

- Try out a unique mix of emotions. Happy to sad, sad to angry, upset to elated.

It doesn't have to be an opposite emotion either, just deviate from the starting emotion to push the chapter ending into must-read-more territory.

Stir Up a Shock

For page-turning, nothing beats a shock. It's almost as good as a cliffhanger ending. With a shock, however, the expectation is that the reader will get a resolution/answer fairly quickly, one that will keep them reading until they find it out.

Brainstorm the shocks that would fit in with your plot, such as...

- An unexpected visitor.

- A sudden death.

- The main character finding out that someone who they thought was dead is still alive.

Make it big, if you can, but limit a shocking shock to one chapter end only to maximize its effectiveness.

A shock every other chapter will wear thin. Be strategic with this option and remember to solve it within the following few chapters to keep the reader happy.

Learn the Value of Vows

Not every chapter of a book needs to be on-the-edge stuff. When you're writing the slower-paced chapters to balance the story or show character development, however, it's easy to wonder how you'll create an ending that makes your reader pick the book up again ASAP.

One option is to use a vow, the kind where a character will declare their intentions for...

- Seeking revenge.

- Protecting those they love.
- Succeeding in their goal.
- Finding an answer.

By declaring a vow in the last sentence, you're making even the slowest of scenes more interesting and sparking the curiosity of your readers, who'll want to find out if the drama of the vow lives up to the hype.

Set Loose a Secret

Secrets drive plots forward, and unleashing a juicy one during the closing paragraphs of the right chapter has the power to keep readers up all night finishing your book.

- Who dropped the mysterious package at the door?
- What was said in the overheard phone call?
- Did everyone but the main character know where their best friend was when the boy next door disappeared?

Close the chapter with the right secret and you'll keep the reader on the hook.

Flip Fortunes

Imagine kicking off the chapter with your main character finally asking out the person they've been interested in forever. They're happy, and readers are happy. The story is going in the direction they want. Then, even before the chapter is over, the fortunes are flipped.

- Cancel the date.
- Steal the painstakingly found treasure.
- Sideline the good news with the baddest of news.

Flipping the fortune of your characters from the start of the chapter to the end is one way to ensure your readers will dive straight into the next chapter. They'll want to see why you messed everything up again when it was just getting so good.

Pose a Question Without an Answer

While a well-placed question can pop up anytime throughout your book, adding one in the very last sentence of a chapter, when no answer can be given, is an ultimate page-turning trick.

Imagine how readers will react when they're reading about the main character being at home waiting for her boyfriend to call, but then the phone rings and the conversation is strange. The reader doesn't know who's on the line and the final sentence is the main character asking who she's talking to (*gasp*). Is it the hospital calling to say her boyfriend has been in an accident? Or is it Ghostface wanting to know her favorite scary movie?

- Add an unanswered question at the end of the chapter that lingers enough for the reader to turn every page to find the answer.

Such a writer's trick is simple yet effective, and when used in just the right chapter, at the right point in your story, it will not only create a great chapter ending, but a good read too.

Related Checklists

The Book Openings Checklist
The Book Endings Checklist

The Chapter Endings Checklist

◯ **Create Conflict**
Add conflict to the last paragraph of the last page of a feel-good chapter.

◯ **Elicit New Emotions**
Deviate from the starting emotion of the chapter at the very end to push the ending into must-read-more territory.

◯ **Stir Up a Shock**
Add a shocking shock to one chapter end only to maximize its effectiveness and remember to solve it within the following few chapters to keep the reader happy.

◯ **Learn the Value of Vows**
For a slower-paced chapter, declare a vow such as the main character deciding to seek revenge, in the last sentence to spark the curiosity of your readers.

◯ **Set Loose a Secret**
Unleashing a juicy secret during the closing paragraphs of the right chapter has the power to keep readers up all night finishing your book.

◯ **Flip Fortunes**
Changing the fortune of your characters from the start of the chapter to the end is one way to ensure your readers will dive straight into the next chapter.

◯ **Pose a Question Without an Answer**
A well-placed question in the very last sentence of a chapter, when no answer can be given, is the ultimate page-turning trick.

The Book Endings Checklist

I'M SURE WE'VE ALL read a book where the buildup to the ending went nowhere. Or worse, ended unresolved, leaving you with more questions than answers.

While endings can be as predictable or as rule-breaking as you want, and I believe the author should always write the book ending *they* want, there are some tried-and-true tips to follow to ensure an ending that won't frustrate readers.

Show the Meaning

No matter what type of book it is and what happens, the end needs to show that everything that happened in the book *had* meaning.

- Was the problem solved?
- Did the characters change?
- Was there justice, even if it wasn't fair?

Prove there was a meaning for the events in the story, no matter whether it's good, bad, indifferent, happy, sad, resolved or open-ended, and use your ending to show that.

Show the Ending

You've given the reader the chance to live as the character throughout the whole book, don't ditch that at the end by *telling* them what happened in the aftermath.

- Show your readers what is happening in the story at the end, don't just tell it to them.

The only exception is if you can't show the loose ends tied up any other way, and need to use a good epilogue.

Shy Away from Anything New

Unless your book is part of a series and new info needs to be introduced at the end to drum up interest for the next book, shy away from anything new.

- Don't spend the final few chapters tying up all the plot strands only to kick off another one.

- Don't reveal something not known before (unless it's a plot twist that makes sense).

- In a standalone story, your final chapter/s should be about bringing everything together and to a close.

- Don't add new characters.

- Don't start a new plot.

- Don't use a new problem to kick off the action again instead of slowing it down to a natural conclusion.

You want your readers closing the book, knowing what happened in your story and being at peace with the ending (regardless of whether it was happy or sad), not throwing your tome across the room because something new happened on the final page and there won't be another book to resolve it. Don't be *that* writer.

Resolve Everything

While cliffhangers have their time and place in a story, and one in the final chapter of an ongoing saga is perfectly fine, if your book is ending—for the sake of readers everywhere—resolve your plot strands!

- It doesn't have to be a happy resolve.

- You don't have to over-explain the resolve, but do resolve things on some level.

- Solve the big mystery.

- Fix every little problem since chapter one.

- Give the readers either straight answers or enough hints they can work out what happened.

Books without a clear resolution are some of the most frustrating—and the last thing you want to do as a writer is annoy your readers.

Drop the Dumb Luck

A coincidence can be used to great effect in a book to kick off the plot, but using a coincidence to end your book... not so much.

- Unless you have set up dumb luck being the way your book ends really, really well from the get-go, *do not* go down that path.

- Readers want to see your characters earn their ending.

- They want the murderer caught because the main character outsmarted them, not because they tripped running away and accidentally triggered an alarm.

Ditch the Way-Too-Happy Ending

As much as readers want to see every character survive, the bad guys get their comeuppance, and the good guys win, that's *not* life, and doesn't make a good story.

Yes, things can go the main character's way and they can end up better at the end than they were at the beginning of the story, but there's always a cost for those things.

- Have a happy ending if it serves the story, but keep it realistic.

Not everyone gets the love of their life. Friendships don't always last, and not every wish turns out perfect.

Make Sure the Main Character Is Active in the Climax

Readers have spent most of the book with your main character, and if you've done your job as a writer, they are attached to them.

- Make sure your main character isn't only observing.
- Don't let things just happen to them or around them during your big ending.
- Have them be active in the climax.
- Ensure they are playing a part in changing the outcome.

Readers want to see your main character win or get what they deserve. If your ending leads to a big climax and the main character is on the sidelines, too passive, or nowhere to be found, the reader will be disappointed.

Save the Highest Stakes Until Last

Stakes drive the story forward and should build toward one big stake that will make or break the main character.

- Keep whatever that stake is until last.
- Bring it to a head so it can be resolved.

For example, kicking off your story with a kidnapping and leaving the rescue until the final chapters with the main character having their big hero moment and the kidnapper getting their comeuppance puts the highest stakes last. Following that same plot but having the rescue occur halfway through the book just sets you up for a fizzer of an ending. What else are you going to fill the final chapters with if the highest stakes have already been and gone?

Save the rescue until the closing chapters and nail that ending.

Evolve the Relationships Between Characters

Just as any relationship in life changes and evolves, so should the relationships between your characters.

- If they meet in the first chapter, they should know each other well by the final.

- Some could be friends at the start of the book and then enemies by the end, or vice versa.

Relationships should change and deepen throughout the course of the book, and you'll want that obvious difference by the closing pages to help create a good ending.

Perfect the Timing of the Resolution

Your final resolution *shouldn't* be something that drags on through the final ten chapters, but it also shouldn't be done and dusted in one page.

- Check that it's satisfying and doesn't finish too quickly.

- If you can't judge how long or short your ending should be, workshop it with some trusted beta readers.

Go With the Right Ending Type

You may know it when you start, it might pop up when outlining, or you could have no clue until you're writing the last chapter, but every book needs an ending, and every writer needs to work out the best kind to use.

- ***Resolved/Tied Up***: The happy-ever-after, tie-it-up-in-a-neat-bow, totally satisfying option.

- ***Cliffhanger/Unresolved***: This one doesn't resolve and leaves readers wanting more via the introduction of a cliffhanger.

- ***Expanded/Epilogue***: The ending where you've resolved the main plot and then use the closing pages to expand the story just a little further, with a *"Three months later..."* type thing, or a flashforward decades ahead.

- ***Circle***: This is where the end of your book starts back at the beginning. This can be a very effective writing trick. Often, something that seemed insignificant or typical at the start of the book can gain new meaning when the story circles back to it.

- ***Ambiguous/Interpretive***: This is the kind of story ending where readers aren't sure what happened. They've been given info that could lead to multiple endings, or been left to make up their own minds. It can be very frustrating for readers when executed poorly.

- ***Combo***: This one combines ending types. Where this option can go wrong is using too many combinations. Your best bet is to stick to two and do them well. For example, a cliffhanger that circles back to the beginning could create an ending that will leave your readers in awe. A cliffhanger that circles back, gives three ambiguous choices, and then an epilogue that only gives closure to one... not so much.

It's frustrating as a reader to be enjoying a book and then have the story fall apart in the final chapter.

This isn't so much about disagreeing with the author's creative choices, but more about whether the end of the book lived up to the promises made about delivering the ending your readers deserve/expect.

Related Checklists

The Stakes Checklist
The Chapter Endings Checklist
The Book Openings Checklist

The Book Endings Checklist

◯ **Show the Meaning**
Use your ending to prove there was a meaning for the events in the story, no matter whether it's good, bad, indifferent, happy, sad, resolved, or open-ended.

◯ **Show the Ending**
Don't tell the readers what happened at the end of your book, show them with your words.

◯ **Shy Away from Anything New**
Avoid starting anything new right at the end of your book (unless it's part of a series and new info *needs* to be introduced to hook readers for the next book).

◯ **Resolve Everything**
If your book is ending for good (no sequels)—for the sake of readers everywhere—resolve every plot strand!

◯ **Drop the Dumb Luck**
Unless you have set up dumb luck being the way your book ends well, do not go down that path. Readers want to see your characters earn their ending.

◯ **Ditch the Way-Too-Happy Ending**
Have a happy ending if it serves the story, but keep it realistic. Not everyone gets the love of their life, friendships don't always last, and not every wish turns out perfect.

The Book Endings Checklist

◯ Make Sure the Main Character Is Active in the Climax
Readers want to see your main character win or get what they deserve. If your ending leads to a big climax and the main character is nowhere to be found, the reader will be disappointed.

◯ Save the Highest Stakes Until Last
Save the rescue until the closing chapters and nail that ending.

◯ Evolve the Relationships Between Characters
Relationships should change and deepen throughout the course of the book, and you'll want that obvious difference in the closing pages.

◯ Perfect the Timing of the Resolution
Your final resolution shouldn't be something that drags on through the final ten chapters, but it also shouldn't be done and dusted in one page.

◯ Go With the Right Ending Type
Every book needs an ending, and every writer needs to work out the best kind to use (see the expanded checklist for types).

Characters

For characters who are distinct, have motivation, and can be described without them having to look at their own reflection in a mirror, look no further than the checklists in this section.

The Distinct Characters Checklist

WHEN IT COMES TO the characters in your book, no one is going to know them like *you* do.

Bringing these imaginary people to life and making them feel real is a tricky art. One that you can master with practice, learned skills, and this checklist.

Don't Make Them Sound the Same

Easier said than done, right? Especially through the first few drafts, when you didn't know them so well and you were just throwing dialogue on the page.

If you can add any character name to dialogue that ends in *he/she said*, and it makes no difference to what's said, then your characters sound the same and you need to do something about it.

- Tailor the dialogue to your characters.

Just as people have their own way of greeting someone (*hi, hello, hey, howdy*), your characters should be given different ways of saying things.

Let's look at these two pieces of dialogue:

"Here is the situation."
"Here's the sitch."

Same words/meaning, but they sound so different. The first belongs to a more formal character, while the second is definitely a character who is laid back, and each has an automatic distinct voice even though they're saying the same thing.

- Aim for differences in dialogue with your characters.

- Throw in action beats that suit each character, i.e. one might always twirl the ends of her hair when talking.

- If you do it well enough, readers should know who is talking just by the dialogue alone, no name attached.

- You need to *know* your characters to get to that level, to pull off exactly how each one would react to the same news.

- If something surprising happens in your story, they can't all say *Oh my god!*

Establish distinctive dialogue that suits the personality of each of your characters and you'll be fine.

Give Them Different Styles

Even though reading about characters isn't as visual as seeing them on a screen, you can still separate their sameness by giving them different styles.

- Hair length.

- Hair color.

- The way they style their hair (always in a ponytail, or always straight), gives distinction.

- Zero in on items of clothing, such as always putting your main character in blue jeans, or long dresses, and other characters in button-down shirts.

Eliminate Similar Names

Does that mean you need to come up with wild names for each character? *No* (unless your book world is sci-fi or fantasy-based).

- Skip giving your characters similar-sounding names

- Ensure none of the names start with the same letter.

Just try to avoid *Glen* and *Glenda* or *Dave* and *David* and you should be okay.

Play Up Different Quirks

You could make these quirks zany for automatic distinction, or to play up something normal.

- The quirk should make your character stand out.

- Limit each individual quirk to an individual character so the reader associates the quirk with them.

- Once such a quirk is established, it sets that character apart from all others.

- You don't need to include crazy mannerisms either, just basic ones, such as one character being the only person in the book who rolls their eyes.

If every character fidgets when they talk, there's nothing to make anyone stand out to the reader, so pick something different for every character and use it for them consistently.

Dig Deep on Their Personalities

If you dig deep into your character's personalities, you can work out their backstories and then give traits that only apply to them.

- How would one character who never worked hard in their life react to starting from scratch?

- How would another character who has had nothing to their name handle a million-dollar lotto win?

- Fill in a detailed character profile to work it out.

- Pen a backstory that *won't* be included in the manuscript so you can work out these details. You knowing such details well enough should naturally show up in your writing without having to explicitly put it on the page.

Just like in real life, where the things that happen to us shape who we become, give the same detail to your characters.

Perfect the Voice

There are some books where the character voice is immediate. If the character voice of the main character is on point from the first sentence, it makes you want to follow their journey.

- Plan how you want your character to be. If you can't do that from the start of your draft, wait until you've finished and then have a good look at what's on the page.

- Define how your character acts, talks, and thinks, and make sure it's coming across for your readers.

Ramp up the Relatability

Infuse your characters with common traits and there's bound to be a reader out there who identifies with them.

- Give them popular interests or hobbies and readers will feel connected.

- If you've got a character who sees every movie under the sun, loves tacos, and owns a cat, I can vouch that myself—and plenty of other readers with those interests—are going to root for them.

- Make your characters as relatable as possible, both in personality, pastimes, hardships, and wins.

It's going to give your readers someone they identify with.

Paint Them in Shades of Gray

People aren't perfect, and your characters shouldn't be either.

- Even heroes need shades of gray to make them believable.

- Yes, your main character can be good, but they also need flaws.

- If all they do is run around winning, there's no tension or reason for the reader to want to go on a journey with them or to care what happens.

Paint your characters in shades of gray—with good and bad flaws.

Back Them up with a Backstory

It's a good idea to give all of your characters some backstory.

- Major characters should have a well-planned and executed story.
- Minor characters can get away with something as simple as a paragraph mentioned in passing.
- Characters who pop up once don't need one.

For your major characters, the backstory can be dripped throughout the book, with anything that mirrors their arc popping up in time to make an event or scene make sense.

For example, a main character who suffered a near-drowning as a child is suddenly forced to enter the water to save a friend. With the backstory of the drowning accident in mind, readers will wonder if they'll hesitate or step up, giving you tension and an interesting character.

Make Them Consistent

Everything your characters do should be in line with the character you establish at the start of the book, and any changes to that character should be something that follows a clear, believable arc.

- If you have a character who's been nothing but a team player in every event of the book and they suddenly don't show up at the big climax, readers will notice.
- Unless you've foreshadowed a good reason this character wouldn't be there, you've ruined their consistency and believability.

No writer wants their book abandoned because of reader frustration, so create characters with consistent and believable actions.

When you combine that with the items listed on this checklist, you'll have no issues creating distinct characters.

Related Checklists

The Backstory Checklist
The Dialogue Tips Checklist
The Describing Without a Mirror Checklist

✓ The Distinct Characters Checklist

◯ **Don't Make Them Sound the Same**
Just as people have their own way of greeting someone (hi, hello, hey, howdy), your characters should be given different ways of saying things.

◯ **Give Them Different Styles**
Separate character sameness by giving them differences, including varied hair length, hair color, hairstyles, and tastes in clothing.

◯ **Eliminate Similar Names**
Avoid Glen and Glenda or Dave and David and you should be okay.

◯ **Play Up Different Quirks/Mannerisms**
If every character fidgets when they talk, there's nothing to make anyone stand out to the reader, so pick something different for every character and use it for them consistently.

◯ **Dig Deep on Their Personalities**
Just like in real life where the things that happen to us shape who we become, give the same detail to your characters.

◯ **Perfect the Voice**
Define how each character acts, talks, and thinks, and make sure it's coming across for your readers.

 The Distinct Characters Checklist

◯ **Ramp up the Relatability**
Make your characters as relatable as possible, both in personality, pastimes, hardships, and wins, and there's bound to be a reader out there who identifies with them.

◯ **Paint Them in Shades of Gray**
People aren't perfect, and your characters shouldn't be either. Give them both good and bad flaws.

◯ **Back Them up with a Backstory**
Major characters should have a well-planned and executed story. Minor characters can get away with something as simple as a paragraph mentioned in passing. Characters who pop up once don't need one.

◯ **Make Them Consistent and Believable**
Everything your characters do should be in line with the character you establish at the start of the book, and any changes to that character should be something that follows a clear, believable arc.

The Character Motivation Checklist

DURING THE PROCESS OF crafting your characters, one important thing to include is motivation.

This isn't just because motivation will get the story moving forward, but because it'll create well-rounded characters, the kind that readers will become invested in and let everyone else know about.

Show Motivation on the Page

Motivation isn't just your character needing to be the hero and save the day, it's *why* they need to be the hero and save the day.

If they're taking off toward danger *just because*, it's not very interesting. If they're heading toward danger because they once failed to act and it resulted in the death of a friend, and *now* they want to save others from the same fate, it's definitely interesting.

- Behind every move of motivation, there should be a solid reason, and that reason should be shown on the page.

- Don't leave your reader to guess why your character is doing something.

- Flesh out the motivation in your backstory using your character's internal thoughts.

- Use a plot twist to reveal why being a hero is so important to them.

Make the Motivation Believable

Just like in life, your characters should want *something*. It's them pursuing that want that will keep your readers turning the page.

- Make their motivation believable.

- Pick a motivation that can be universal at a base level, and you've got a hook readers will want to cling to.

Not every reader will relate to your character wanting a silver locket necklace, but them wanting that necklace because it's the same as one their mother owned before she mysteriously disappeared is definitely something relatable.

It might not be a necklace for the reader, but the motivation to own something the same as a beloved parent can be a shared, believable want. The necklace is irrelevant, but the motivation to own something the same as a lost loved one isn't.

Combine Motivation with Conflict

One of the best ways to make motivation work in your story is to combine it with conflict, such as...

- Outside conflict with other characters.

- Bad situations.

- Internal conflict that your character is struggling with.

- Multiple conflicts where your characters struggle can reveal a lot about them, making them human and relatable.

- Dealing with multiple conflicts adds tension, suspense, and doesn't make things too easy, i.e. boring.

Your characters digging deep to overcome their conflicts is what readers want to see, so infuse the motivation with as much conflict as the story allows.

Payoff the Motivation

Readers haven't followed your characters from page one just to see everything that had driven them forward not be resolved.

If a story shows a character using motivation to change, but it's not paid off with them triumphing over their fears or being the hero, it makes for a flat, dissatisfying ending.

- Conclude any motivation correctly.

Giving the motivation the payoff the characters, story, and readers deserve will give you an interesting, satisfying ending—which is something all writers and readers want.

Related Checklists

The Payoff Checklist
The Conflict Checklist
The Distinct Characters Checklist

The Character Motivation Checklist

○ **Show Motivation on the Page**
Behind every move of motivation, there should be a solid reason, and that reason should be shown on the page.

○ **Make the Motivation Believable**
Pick a motivation that can be universal at a base level, and you've got a hook readers will want to cling to.

○ **Combine Motivation with Conflict**
Dealing with multiple conflicts adds tension, suspense, and doesn't make things too easy, i.e. boring.

○ **Payoff the Motivation**
If your character's motivation changes them but it's not paid off with a triumph over their fears, it creates a dissatisfying ending.

The Describing Without a Mirror Checklist

JUST AS BOOK TRENDS see certain genres fall in and out of favor, there are certain elements of books that once worked but now don't.

One example is the clichéd mirror look—aka when the author has a character look in a mirror/mirrored surface and describe themselves so the reader knows what they look like.

Yep, writers used to do this *all the time*, and when you're a wannabe writer and see this trick used in the big-time published books, it works its way into your own writing.

There are better options, though, and they're in this checklist.

Through the Lens of Other Characters

This, of course, only works if your book uses multiple POVs. If it does, have the other characters do the heavy description-lifting and bring your main character/other characters to life on the page.

- Put in observations from other characters about how the main character/everyone else looks.

To show this, we're going to be using our Jenny and Carla example characters. For what follows, Carla will be our main character and Jenny is our secondary POV character.

Example:

Carla was coming toward her now, **her auburn curls** swept up in the winter breeze and whipping their way across **her round face**. Jenny could already see the chill adding a pink glow to **Carla's bronzed cheeks**, which were pushed high by her gigantic smile.
"Why are you in such a good mood?" How was this the same person who spent last night wallowing in her hot chocolate?

Using POV Inner Dialogue

If your only POV is the main character, or you need their physical description added *before* a different character's POV can describe them...

- Work the physical description in with main character inner dialogue/thoughts.

- Try to ensure these type of internal thoughts sound natural and arise in the right situation. You want the reader to pick up on the physical description without being pulled out of the story because the main character decides during a pivotal moment to list every feature of their face.

Example:

Orange wasn't the right color to blend with **Carla's bronzed skin**, and the fit wasn't exactly flattering to **her curves**. *Or my arms.* She tugged on the jumper's right sleeve, sighing when it barely covered half of her **long wrist**. But Jenny had given her the jumper and would be devastated if she didn't wear it to her birthday party.

In this example, you get a sense of what Carla looks like with descriptive words and her own internal thoughts, and it's happening as she's getting dressed, which is a natural place in the story for her to muse about her physical features.

Harnessing the Reactions of Others

If you don't want to use inner thoughts to spell out every physical description...

- Work in character description via the *reactions* of other characters.

Example:

"Carla? Is that you?" A blond with a chirpy voice squealed in Carla's ear before she'd squeezed all the way through the front door.
"Yes?" She tried to place the excited face staring at her, but couldn't.
"You look amazing! That jumper goes perfectly with **your auburn hair**."
My hair? "Ahh, Lola. From the hair salon downtown, right?"

Describing Family Traits

Another great way to slip your main character's description in is by...

- Having them describe their family traits.

Example:

Carla had towered over her mother since she was eleven, which was unusual since everyone else in her family was **on the short side. She and her mom still shared the same eye color**, though. **Bright green with flecks of gold** that always got them compliments.

With Physical Actions

And the final tip for getting some character description into your sentences is by...

- Using physical actions. Here, we learn about the height of both Jenny and Carla.

Example:

Jenny rose on her tippy-toes to reach the good glasses at the back of the cupboard and swung the door open so wide she almost hit Carla in the face. "Sorry. Maybe you should have gotten the glasses. **You don't need a ladder to reach anything above bench-level** in this kitchen."
Carla grinned, her **long arm** effortlessly reaching for the inner cupboard. "You know I'm always happy to help **you shorties out**."

As you can see, there are lots of fun ways to add character descriptions without a cliché in sight. Done with the right wording, your readers will effortlessly put together a picture in their mind without being pulled off the page by your main character stopping to look in a mirror.

Related Checklists

The Internal Thoughts Checklist
The Action Beats Checklist

✓ The Describing Without a Mirror Checklist

◯ **Through the Lens of Other Characters**
Use other characters to do the heavy description-lifting with observations about how the main character/other characters look.

◯ **Using POV Inner Dialogue/Thoughts**
When it's just one POV, work the physical description of them into your book with inner dialogue/thoughts instead of having them look in a mirror.

◯ **Harnessing the Reactions of Others**
Having a character exclaim their love of your main character's auburn-colored hair effortlessly lets the reader know about your main character's physical description.

◯ **Describing Family Traits**
Slip your main character's description in by having them describe their family traits, i.e. comparing their eye color with their mother's.

◯ **With Physical Actions**
The physical actions of your characters can add physical info about them. A short main character has to rise on tippy-toes to reach something high, letting the reader know they're vertically challenged.

Scenes

The checklists in this section will make your book scenes pop by letting you know what to establish, how to make the most of action scenes, using sequels to complement your scenes, and what to do when you just can't get a scene to work.

The What to Establish in a Scene Checklist

UNLESS YOU'RE A SUPER-ORGANIZED planner who sticks to their writing outline religiously, there will be a point during the writing process when you'll come to a scene and not know where to start to make sure it includes everything you need it to.

Luckily for you, there are some routine scene elements that can be established, and using this checklist will allow you to do that.

The Character Point of View

If you're working with a first-person, single character, this doesn't really apply. If you're working with multiple character POVs and/or in third-person, then it does.

- One of the first things your scene should establish is whose POV it's coming from.

You might have read books where the author puts the name of the character at the top of the chapter, or you could do what I do, which is to make sure it's obvious in the opening sentence of the paragraph who the main character/POV of the scene is. This can be achieved through either dialogue or description.

Examples: (*Taken from Blackbirch: The Dark Half*)

Descriptions:
Kallie fell sideways, her shoulder taking the brunt as the stony surface pressed into her flesh. The rocks also did a number on her temple, the whiplash splintering across her forehead. She rolled onto her back, wincing as the ice water filled her clothes. Her head twisted to the side; her view tainted by brunette waves, moist

with a warm redness that stuck to her skin. She raised chilled fingers to push the strands away.

Dialogue:
"That's him." **Kallie** tapped her finger against the foggy glass of the van's windshield. "That's the guy I saw." She kept her eyes on Kered Wheeler as he left the Curvers Rock Security office and there was no doubt in her mind. This was the man her vision showed had energy capable of pulling off an attack like the one in the woods.

In these examples, *Kallie*, is mentioned in the very first sentence of the scene, establishing her at the POV character.

The Places and Settings

This won't be relevant for scenes where the setting or place is already known, but if your scene has switched location and is taking place somewhere that hasn't already been established, then that detail needs to be included.

Establish places and settings with...

- Descriptions
- Dialogue.
- Action beats.

Try and add this info early in the scene to avoid confusion for the reader.

Example: (*Taken from Blackbirch: The Beginning*)

Emerging from the **dead trees** was like shifting from night to day, only it wasn't the sun's rays greeting them. *What is this?* Eve blinked, trying to force her eyes to adjust. She found herself bathed in a light unlike anything she'd seen before. It settled over the illuminated area like a mist, yet showered the dirt and branches it touched with a muted dullness.

In this example, the POV character, *Eve*, has started the scene by entering a dead section of forest in the Blackbirch woods. The first line establishes that with a simple "dead trees" reference. You can be as detailed or as sparse about the place/setting as you need to be, just as long as it establishes for the reader where the characters are in the scene.

The Time/Day/Night

If it's not already known and is relevant to the story, remember to establish time.

Make it clear...

- If it's been hours, days, weeks, or years since the last scene.
- If it's day or night.

Example: (*Taken from Blackbirch: The Dark Half*)

It'd been **hours** since he'd gone to meet Kallie. Sarah twisted her bottom lip with her free hand, her gaze flickering between the grandfather clock in the reading area of the store and the bay window. Each ray of orange sunlight imprinting in the **pink sunset** sky added to her paranoia.

In this example, it's established that hours had passed from the previous scene and that it's the end of the day with the nod to the pink sunset. These little details can easily be added with a few words, or a longer descriptive paragraph if it suits.

Not every scene needs to establish the time or if it's day or night, but it's a good idea to include these details somewhere in the book to make it realistic and to help the reader work out/keep track of when things are happening.

The Characters Present

This is probably the easiest key thing to establish because it'll be obvious from character interactions and dialogue.

Keep in mind that...

- Knowing which characters are in a scene *doesn't* have to be established right away, but try to make it a natural revelation in any given scene.

- You gain nothing by pulling a reader out of a story because a line of dialogue from side character #3 pops up and it wasn't properly signaled that they were even in the scene.

Example: *(Taken from Blackbirch: The Dark Half)*

Josh stepped aside, allowing **Kallie** to move ahead of him into the lamp-lit living room. "**Sarah** must be home." He pointed to the brighter lights of the kitchen. As they got closer to the wide doorway, a murmur of voices floated toward them, carried on the scent of herbs and a burst of hot steam. Josh felt the temperature shift as soon as they stepped into the room and sighed. Finally, the chill of the clearing left his bones. **Grace** stood at the stove, dropping pasta into a pot of bubbling water, and it made him question what time it was. She was rarely home early enough to cook.

In this example, we've got Josh, Kallie, Sarah, and Grace. Josh is the POV character and Kallie is signaled in the scene by him allowing her to move ahead. Sarah is established by Josh's dialogue mention of her, and Grace is made known when Josh and Kallie notice her in the kitchen. As you can see, it doesn't take much to let the reader know which characters to expect in a scene and the info can be slotted in effortlessly.

Related Checklists

The POV Checklist
The Settings Checklist
The Dialogue Tips Checklist
The Action Beats Checklist

✓ The What to Establish in a Scene Checklist

◯ **The Character Point of View**
One of the first things your scene should establish is whose POV it's coming from using either descriptions or dialogue.

◯ **The Places and Settings**
Establish places and settings with descriptions, dialogue, and action beats as early as you can to avoid confusion.

◯ **The Time/Day/Night**
When relevant, make it clear it's been hours, days, weeks, or years since the last scene, and/or if it's day or night.

◯ **The Characters Present**
Establish who is in the scene with character interactions and dialogue, making it a natural revelation when needed, and not necessary as soon as the scene begins.

The Scene Sequel Checklist

If you haven't heard of scene sequels before, be ready to have your world rocked, or at the very least, learn that there is another meaning for the word sequel in the writing world.

A sequel, in regards to scenes, is the smaller scene *after* a big scene that allows both the characters and the reader to process what just happened.

You might already do this, you smart cookie, or you could be organically writing sequels and not realizing it's a thing—in which case we can share a cookie—and the following checklist.

Answer the Questions Asked

The key to a good book scene is an event that features (among other things)...

- Plot advancement.
- Character insights.
- Conflict.
- Tension.
- A goal.
- A cliffhanger ending.

What your sequel should feature is *the answer* to these things.

- If you've **advanced the plot**, what is the reaction to the events?

- If you've offered a **character insight**, does it change the relationship between characters?

- If there's **conflict**, what is the outcome of it?

- **Tension** between characters? How do they feel about it?

- Your main character finally achieved their **goal**? What is their reaction?

- The chapter ended on the **cliffhanger** arrival of a mysterious character. The sequel is where you bring home the reveal.

Simply put—your scene is the question and your sequel is the answer.

Provide a Place to Breathe

Sequels are also breathing room. If you've been putting your characters through hell, use your sequel...

- As a respite to the madness.

- As a time to be quiet before the next storm.

Keep In Mind That Everything Has a Purpose

Every scene benefits from moving the plot forward and teaching the reader something about your characters, and sequels are no different.

They should...

- Show the reaction/consequence/outcome of the events of the scene/s before it.

If it doesn't, reevaluate the purpose of your sequel.

Implement a Pattern

If you're a planner or a pantser who dabbles in a bit of structure and guidance, alternating between scenes and sequels should be right up your alley.

To follow a scene/sequel pattern...

- Get the reader on the edge (scene).
- Tease them with some resolve (sequel).
- Up the ante again (scene).
- Give them a moment to catch their breath (sequel).
- Bring things to a head with the climax (scene).
- Finish things with a resolved ending (final sequel).

Not every book has to follow such a strict pattern, however, and you may find that your story works better by spacing out the sequels and hitting the reader with several scenes in a row instead. Decide what works best for you and your story.

Perfect the Pacing

Once you've worked out what pattern you're going with, look at your pacing.

- An action story will need short, fast-paced chapters to keep the reader interested, which means more scenes than sequels.
- On the other end of the spectrum, a character-driven story will enjoy the breathing room and slower pace of sequels mixed with fewer faster-paced scenes.

If you're worried you'll throw your pacing off by slowing down the story just to add a sequel, know that a sequel *doesn't* have to be an entire chapter. It can simply be a paragraph or sentence at the end of a scene.

Include Effects

The sequel is your opportunity to show the effects of everything you've caused.

Killed the main character's family? Got him fired from his job? Had him come home to find his dog has run away? The only way you're a bigger monster than most is if you write these things happening and *don't* follow up with their effects on the main character.

If these events were to happen and they aren't addressed, either pushing the main character into action, making him grow as a person, or revealing his inner devastation, your book is about a character who has a run of bad luck with no lessons learned.

- Show the effects of your scenes. It's the string that pulls your plot together.

- Including the effects makes your book whole and ensures your characters are treated with care, no matter what you throw at them.

- It respects your readers, who also deserve to feel the after-effects of your scenes in the sequels.

Without showing the effects in your sequels, your story is just a bunch of random scenes, not a tightly woven plot. Avoid that outcome by pairing your scene with the right sequel, and you've definitely earned yourself a cookie.

Related Checklists

The Tension Checklist
The Chapter Endings Checklist
The Scene Isn't Working Checklist

The Scene Sequel Checklist

◯ **Answer the Questions Asked**

Your scene sequel should provide the answer to the questions proposed in the scenes before it, so ask yourself the following and implement the answers in your sequels...

- If you've advanced the plot, what is the reaction to the events?
- If you've offered a character insight, does it change the relationship between characters?
- If there's conflict, what is the outcome of it?
- Tension between characters? How do they feel about it?
- Your main character finally achieved their goal? What is their reaction?
- The chapter ended on the cliffhanger arrival of a mysterious character. The sequel is where you bring home the reveal.

◯ **Provide a Place to Breathe**

Sequels give breathing room, a respite to the madness, and are a time to be quiet before the next storm.

◯ **Keep In Mind That Everything Has a Purpose**

Sequels should show the reaction/consequence/outcome of the events of the scene/s before it.

The Scene Sequel Checklist

○ **Implement a Pattern**
If you need guidance, follow a scene/sequel pattern...

- Get the reader on the edge (scene).
- Tease them with some resolve (sequel).
- Up the ante again (scene).
- Give them a moment to catch their breath (sequel).
- Bring things to a head with the climax (scene).
- Finish things with a resolved ending (final sequel).

○ **Perfect the Pacing**
A fast-paced book needs more snappy scenes than slow sequels, whereas slower/character-driven stories need more breathing room sequels.

○ **Include Effects**
The sequel is your opportunity to show the effects of everything you've caused during your scenes, so include them.

The Action Scene Checklist

WHETHER YOUR BOOK IS full of action scenes, or requires just one, getting the balance right is a skill worthy of any writer, and can be achieved with this simple checklist.

Make Every Action Scene Unique

If you have more than one action scene in your book, set them apart.

Even if your main character is coming up against the same foe every time (and especially if they are), play each scene out differently...

- Put it in a different setting.
- Include different kinds of banter.
- If your characters have already enacted the clichéd monologue about plans for world domination, don't repeat it when they meet again before the big finale.
- Try to have unique action. A car chase is thrilling when it's described once, but after the third time, it gets boring.

Ramp up the Realism

For most action, it's a good idea to keep it realistic.

- Use the rules of whatever world your characters are in, whether that's our modern world, historic times, on a distant planet, or a world totally of your own making.

- If you've seen any of the last few *Fast and Furious* movies, you'll know what it means when action fails to stay in the realm of reality. When cars are used as parachutes out of airplanes, it's hard to take the action seriously.

- Remember that unrealistic action risks pulling the reader out of the story/world.

If you find yourself thinking there's no way a character would walk away from this uninjured/alive, look at the realism and ramp it up.

Keep It Short and Snappy

Action scenes work when the pace is quick. Do this by…

- Limiting character movements/descriptions within an action scene. We don't need to know about every nod of a head or reach of hands.

- Ensuring your characters are only saying what's absolutely necessary. It isn't likely a hero in the middle of a challenging sword fight is going to explain his life story while fending off blades.

With everything kept short and snappy, your pacing will automatically work for an action scene, moving the reader along and not slowing things down when they should be racing ahead.

Let the Reader Fill In Details

You don't need to describe every detail of the setting for the action scene to be thrilling for the reader.

- Stopping to describe every inch of the haunted mansion the protagonists have wandered into will ruin the action.

- Pare your details back to atmospheric word choices and let the reader's imagination fill in the rest.

Give them the credit to take cues from what you *do* describe and leave room for the action to be the focus.

Balance with a Non-Action Sequel

Unless you're writing a non-stop action story—and even if you are—you need to balance all that action out.

- Follow your action scenes with a non-action sequel.

In a nutshell, a non-action sequel is where your characters and the reader decompress. It's the low after the high and a chance to slow the story and let everyone catch their breath.

That doesn't mean you have to take things to a boring crawl, just avoid more high octane stuff to make the action you have stand out.

Make Things Clear

There's nothing worse than reading an action scene and not being able to work out what's going on.

At a minimum, make the following crystal clear to your readers...

- Where characters are standing.
- Who is present.
- Where the scene takes place.

If you're not sure yourself, sketch out a diagram of the space and where your characters are standing and plan things out in steps:

1) Villain enters through the back door.

2) Main character is in the kitchen.

3) Side character is coming down the stairs.

Map out in your mind where everyone starts and where they move as the scene progresses. Once it's all visualized and planned in steps, write out the action scene as basically as possible before rewriting to fill in the details.

When you think you've got it, ask someone else to read the scene to see if it makes sense, and then keep refining it until the action plays out clearly and is written in the right style for your book.

Avoid Too Much Staging

When you're planning the action out in steps, it's very easy to go overboard on the staging.

For example, that villain sneaking in the back door is not a sequence that needs to be laid out step-by-step.

The reader doesn't need to know that they cupped a gloved hand over the doorknob, opened the door slowly, stepped one foot forward and then the other, and so on. This drags the scene out. Action scenes need to be snappy. *The villain nudges the back door open and creeps silently into the empty dining room* is usually enough to orientate the reader and get things moving.

- Check that staging is minimal.
- Keep things snappy.
- Orientate the reader as simply, clearly, and early as possible.

Add Realistic Injuries

If your scene is all about action, chances are there will be injuries. They don't have to be fatal, but they have to be realistic in regard to what's happening.

If your side character coming down the stairs runs into your villain, turns to go back up the stairs, but is knocked down, they've gotten themselves an injury.

It could be as basic as them momentarily falling on the stairs, hitting their shins, but being able to bounce up and get away from the danger. They may have a slight limp as they run back up the stairs, but within a minute, those sore shins would have recovered, save for some bruising the next day.

Or the hit from the villain could be bad. They may have a baseball bat that they clobber the side character with. Their fall into the stairs would likely involve a bleeding head injury and fractured ribs from a bigger landing against the stair edges. The side character could then have trouble breathing. They're dizzy, and blood is dripping into their eyes. They may only get halfway up the stairs, gasping for breath as they go.

Whatever injury happens in an action scene...

- Keep it realistic to the situation and circumstances.

Don't Ignore the Impact of Injuries

In the above example, the version of the side character with hurt shins will get away. Their injuries aren't severe, they are pumped full of adrenaline, and they can get up those stairs. Baseball bat injured side character... not so much.

They aren't getting very far with their injuries. The cracked ribs are making it hard to take a breath, their head is pounding, and they're confused and not thinking clearly. If you have them running up the stairs and getting away just as easily as the barely injured side character, you need to rethink the impact of your injuries.

- Avoid the scary movie cliché of characters being stabbed and then walking around in the next scene as if they received a paper cut instead of a life-altering wound.
- Make the impact of the injuries felt.
- If it's serious, write it as serious.

In the real world, big wounds slow people down, and it should be the same for your fictional world too.

Make Your Main Character Active

Even if the situation your main character is in isn't their fault, having them in the middle of an action scene, watching while everything is happening around them instead of being active is pretty boring.

They may not be a fighter, and they may be tied up, but if they aren't actively taking part in the scene, why are they there?

- The main character is the star of the story and should be helping other characters, planning an escape, or plotting what to do next.

- Even if the action scene calls for them to be bested by the villain, the main character should be active in their own defeat.

When that villain comes through the back door, takes out the side character coming down the stairs, and then comes face-to-face with the main character in the kitchen, that main character should be appropriately reacting to the events, not just standing there while it happens around them.

Have them ready with their own weapon after hearing through the wall what is happening on the stairs. Even if they're scared and looking for a place to hide, show them scrambling to fit into a pantry.

Use the Five Senses

An action scene isn't just about the moves the characters make, it's what they see, smell, taste, touch, and hear.

Let's continue using the last scenario as our example. The main character hears the commotion on the stairs and knows the side character is hurt and they are next. The main character could keep listening to gauge when the villain is close by. That's one sense ticked off right there.

Now, the main character is panicking. The bowl of food they're holding shakes in their trembling hands. It's tomato soup, a comfort food they were preparing as a distraction, and now it will be their undoing.

They drop the bowl. The noise alerts the villain that there's someone in the kitchen. The touch of the hot soup on the main character's hand causes them pain and more sound as they cry out before shoving their hand in their mouth to stifle the noise. They taste the tangy soup on their tongue as the rest of the liquid drops from the bowl to the floor, causing the main character to almost slip as they run to the pantry to hide. They make it inside as the villain enters the room.

The villain can't see the main character, but they can smell the soup. They walk around the kitchen counter and see the mess on the floor, and the red, sloppy footprints leading to the main character's hiding place.

Use...

- Sound.

- Touch.

- Taste.

- Smell.

- Sight.

They will drive the action forward and add depth to your scene.

Pairing a writer's trick like the five senses should fill your scenes with all the elements you'll need to pull off any action, even a baseball bat-welding villain interrupting a dinner of comforting tomato soup.

Related Checklists

The Settings Checklist
The Scene Sequel Checklist
The Stage Direction Checklist
The Five Senses Checklist

The Action Scene Checklist

○ **Make Every Action Scene Unique**
Even if your main character comes up against the same foe every time, play each scene with a different setting, banter, and unique action.

○ **Ramp up the Realism**
Use the rules of whatever world your characters are in (modern, historic times, a distant planet, or a made-up world) to keep the action realistic.

○ **Keep It Short and Snappy**
Limit character movements/descriptions and ensure they're only saying what's necessary.

○ **Let the Reader Fill In Details**
Use atmospheric word choices and let the reader's imagination fill in the rest.

○ **Balance with a Non-Action Sequel**
Follow your action scenes with a non-action sequel where your characters decompress.

○ **Make Things Clear**
Sketch a diagram of the space, where your characters are standing, and plan things out in steps before writing the scene.

The Action Scene Checklist

◯ **Avoid Too Much Staging**
Check that staging is minimal, keep things snappy, and orientate the reader as simply, clearly, and early as possible.

◯ **Add Realistic Injuries**
Whatever injury happens, keep it realistic to the situation and circumstances.

◯ **Don't Ignore the Impact Of Injuries**
Avoid the scary movie cliché of characters being stabbed and then walking around as if they received a paper cut. If it's a serious injury, write it as serious.

◯ **Make Your Main Character Active**
The main character is the star of the story and should be helping others, planning an escape, or plotting what to do next. Even if the action scene calls for them to be bested by the villain, the main character should be active in their own defeat.

◯ **Use the Five Senses**
An action scene isn't just about the moves the characters make, it's also about what they see, smell, taste, touch, and hear.

The Scene Isn't Working Checklist

BOOKS ARE BUILT ON scenes, those lovely little snapshots that move the plot forward, give the traits of your characters time to shine, and provide the backbone of your story. They're important to the book, which is why it's important to get them right.

But even on the best writing days, sometimes those scenes just *don't* work. There are writing rules that state if a scene isn't working, cut it.

That might work if losing the scene isn't pivotal, but if it is, then you'll have to take that pace-slowing piece and make changes. If you're not sure where to start, the tips in this checklist should help.

Change the POV

This tip is for books written from multiple points of view.

- If the scene isn't coming off on the page as you'd hoped, trying switching the POV to another character.

Just writing from a different perspective could give the scene what it needs to work.

Change the Setting

Say your book involves characters discussing a murder. They could be having such a conversation huddled in a car parked on the street in broad daylight, trying to look casual, just two people chatting away while the sun shines down and the noise of daily life drowns out the darkness of their conversation.

Now imagine that same conversation on a dark, moonless night where they've met to discuss the crime at an abandoned building. It's cliché, but the different setting immediately transforms the scene into something more befitting of the characters' conversation.

- If you find your scene isn't working, change the setting to something that'll give the scene more weight.

Add Characters

While you don't want a scene overflowing with characters, sometimes introducing another may be just what it needs.

Adding another character to a stilted scene can lead to...

- A different dynamic.
- Change the course of your characters' actions.
- Give more insight to a detailed conversation.
- Take your scene in a different direction.

I've written several scenes where just putting in another character has led to a plot twist I hadn't planned, which really helped to move the story along nicely.

Take Characters Away

On the flip side, taking away excess characters can give you a tighter scene.

If you go back to our murder discussion example, imagine if there were three people that night who were all involved in what happened. It would make sense for them to meet up to discuss the event, huddled together under that dark sky, with the abandoned building creaking when the wind blows.

The three could be fighting over what they've done—or you could write one character out of the scene. Suddenly the two left are plotting instead of fighting, working out a way to put the blame on the now removed third character.

- Take away one or more characters.

It makes for a more interesting scene, and you've got yourself a new plot twist too.

Ask What-If?

Asking yourself what would happen if a certain event did or didn't take place is a great way to create a story or expand on a plot. Applying this same question to a scene that's not working does the same thing.

What if your main character didn't go to school or work today? What if they opened a wrongly delivered parcel? What if they arrived somewhere too early or too late? How would that change the events of the scene?

- Ask What-if? for your non-working scene and brainstorm different answers to the question.

It'll kick-start your creativity and could take the scene from run-of-the-mill to interesting.

Skip the Yadda-Yadda

Sometimes the reason a scene is lacking is because you yadda-yadda'd the best part.

Maybe you couldn't be bothered to write it properly. Maybe you didn't know how to write it properly. Or maybe you didn't know how important the scene would be when you created the first draft. In any case, you've got a scene that's not working because the *only* interesting thing about it hasn't been given enough detail.

- Skip the yadda-yadda and see where you can delve a little deeper with internal character thoughts, description, or conflict.

On the flip side, maybe you've gone *too* detailed and dragged the scene out.

- Take a good look at every sentence and see if transforming some paragraphs *into* yadda-yadda will get the scene moving.

Tell, Just a Little

Another piece of well-known writing advice is showing and not telling. That means instead of telling the reader how the main character outsmarted her foe or what emotions she's feeling as she does it, you show it. Where such advice doesn't work in a scene is taking it too far and showing *everything*.

Does the reader want to read about the big magical battle, feeling how the main character felt when power coursed through his veins? *Yes!*

Do they want to read about how the main character got to said battle in his beat-up old car, parked it down the road and walked on tired, aching feet to the place of the battle? *No!*

You might have to include that stuff because the car or setting is relevant in the grand scheme of the story, but that is info that *can* be told, not shown.

- Examine your scene for parts the reader needs to know but can be *told*.

- *Show* the bits the reader won't want to skim to get your scene working.

Dial-up the Dialogue

There are a few ways to get vital info across to the reader, including a description-filled paragraph or internal character thoughts. I've done this in certain scenes and almost fallen asleep reading them back. Sometimes, it just doesn't work, but one way to get off the train to snooze-ville is by hitching a ride to dialogue town.

- Take that vital, need-to-know info and transform it into a conversation instead.

If you've got at least two characters in the scene and that paragraph where your main character internally muses about something that happened to them can instead be revealed in a snappy back-and-forth conversation, try it and see if it helps your scene to work.

Related Checklists

The POV Checklist
The Settings Checklist
The Distinct Characters Checklist
The Dialogue Checklist

 The Scene Isn't Working Checklist

○ **Change the POV**
If the scene isn't coming off on the page as you'd hoped, try switching the Point of View to another character.

○ **Change the Setting**
Check if it's the setting that's not working by changing it to something that suits/reflects what's going on in the story during the time of the scene.

○ **Add Characters**
Adding another character to a stilted scene can lead to a different dynamic, change the course of your characters' actions, give more insight to a detailed conversation, or take your scene in a different direction.

○ **Take Characters Away**
On the flip side, taking away excess characters can give you a tighter scene.

The Scene Isn't Working Checklist

◯ **Ask What-If?**
Brainstorm some What-ifs? for the stuck scene and see if the answers unstick it.

◯ **Skip the Yadda-Yadda**
Skip the yadda-yadda and see where you can delve a little deeper with internal character thoughts, description, and conflict, or pare back a dragged-out scene to get everything working.

◯ **Tell, Just a Little**
Examine your scene for parts the reader needs to know but can be told, and show the bits the reader won't want to skim.

◯ **Dial-up the Dialogue**
If it works for the scene, take any vital, need-to-know info and transform it into a conversation between characters instead. A snappy back-and-forth conversation may be just what the scene needs.

The Art of Editing

Once you've written your words, it's time to edit them! The checklists in this section will help you see your author blind spots, let you know what to cut so you're not repeating the same info, telling, or staging too much, teach you how to review your manuscript when it's written, and the benefits of penning yourself an edit letter.

The Early Draft Cuts Checklist

THERE'S A REASON IT'S a good idea to not show anyone early drafts, and that's because it's usually full of writing that should be cut.

And these cuts aren't darlings (writing that's good but doesn't fit the story), they're the parts of your manuscript that will make it stronger once you've removed them.

They are the weak words that sneak in and clutter up your sentences, the passages that water down your reveals, the ideas that helped you get those early drafts written, but should now be taken out. Cuts such as...

The Repeats

The repeats are words you use excessively. Usually ones you don't even know you're repeatedly using until it's pointed out by a well-intentioned beta reader (or three or four).

Check for common repeats, like...

- That.
- Realized.
- Surprise.
- See *The Repeats Checklist* for more.

In early drafts, my characters are always realizing things and finding themselves surprised. If you have just ~~realized~~ noticed you have the same issue, put together a repeat list and use your *find/search* function to narrow in and make cuts.

The Author Guide

Early drafts are perfect for working out the story. That's one of their main purposes; to take that nugget of an idea and turn it into a full-blown book. When you're piecing together that jigsaw, the first person you need to tell that story to is yourself.

I'm sure if you look closely at your first few drafts, you'll find the same ideas repeated throughout, similar reveals in different chapters, and the same backstory said in different ways popping up all over the place.

These instances happen when you're working out the plot. It's your *first-draft-self* giving *future-draft-you* a guide for how the story should play out. You need to know those things to finish the adventure. But once the guide is in place, you need to cut up the road map that got you there.

Look for the places where you've...

- Dropped the same backstory.
- Written similar character descriptions.
- Repeated settings.
- Foreshadowed something more than necessary.
- Anything else that gives the same info again and again.

Study each instance, decide what was written better and where it should be placed in the plot for maximum impact, and delete the rest.

Dialogue Tags

Not all dialogue tags need to be cut, but if you spent your early draft typing "he/she said" after every sentence of speech, it's time to learn how much cleaner your draft can be.

- If it's obvious who is speaking, cut names.
- Try using an action beat instead of "said" for the twentieth time.

Non-Character Voice

Writing in a way that puts the reader inside the character's head, making them feel what the main character feels, is no easy feat. It's a skill that takes many drafts to master. That's why your early drafts are bound to be littered with paragraphs that come from a voice that isn't your character's.

- Cut any section of your book that sounds like an instruction manual rather than a real person.

- Look for any piece of dialogue that is so generic any character could have said it. It's not coming from the character voice and should be cut or rewritten in the character's correct voice.

Tells

When writing your early drafts, you might have been under a deadline, or so inspired to get everything down, it was easier to *tell* now and leave the *show* for later. That means the draft you're looking at now is likely a tell-fest and needs some show inserted to make it better.

- Look for telling occurrences.

Cut, rewrite, and turn those telling paragraphs into an imagery-inducing delight.

Staging

Staging is those passages of text where you think it's a good idea to detail *Every. Single. Movement.*

Look for...

- A character crossing a room.

- A character getting out of their car.

- Specifying that the left hand picked up a glass.

- Stating exactly where the characters are standing/sitting/taking a breath.

Unless is it necessary to the plot that the reader knows it's a five-step stroll from the main character's living room to the kitchen, cut it.

Yes, the reader needs an idea of where characters are positioned in a scene and what they're doing, but they don't need *all* the details in between.

The Placeholders

Can't think of a decent name for a character or location in your novel? Stuck on the bridging scene between two action-packed plot twists and decided two filler sentences would do?

Have you ever noted *add more here* and left it at that? Or failed to properly name your characters, because even in a fantasy novel, *NameLater* isn't a good moniker.

These placeholders are a rite of passage when writing an early draft and should always be on your list of cuts to replace with more detail.

- Cut placeholders.

If you've recognized any of these cuts in your own WIP, try removing and/or rewriting and you should end up with a stronger draft. After that, you'll still need copious amounts of edits and chocolate sacrifices to your muse to create a finished draft, but that's a problem for *future-draft-you*.

Related Checklists

The Repeats Checklist
The Dialogue Tips Checklist
The Stage Direction Checklist
The Show Don't Tell Checklist
The Author Blind Spot Checklist

The Early Draft Cuts Checklist

◯ The Repeats
Cut words you know that you use excessively, as well as...

- That.
- Realized.
- Surprise.
- Anything else listed on The Repeats Checklist.

◯ The Author Guide
This is your first-draft-self giving future-draft-you a guide for how the story should play out, but once the guide is in place, cut up the road map. Look for the places where you've...

- Dropped the same backstory.
- Written similar character descriptions.
- Repeated settings.
- Foreshadowed something more than necessary.
- Anything else that gives the same info again and again.

Study each instance, decide what was written better and where it should be placed in the plot for maximum impact, and delete the rest.

◯ Dialogue Tags
Clean up your draft by removing some of your dialogue tags.

- If it's obvious who is speaking, cut names.
- If you can throw in an action beat instead of using "he said" for the twentieth time, do it.

The Early Draft Cuts Checklist

○ **Non-Character Voice**

Early drafts are littered with paragraphs that come from a voice that isn't just right.

- Cut any section of your book that sounds like an instruction manual rather than a real person.
- Look for any piece of dialogue that is so generic any character could have said it and rewrite it into the correct character voice.

○ **Tells**

Getting the story down quickly in an early draft usually means a tell-fest and needs some show inserted to make it better.

- Look for telling occurrences.
- Cut, rewrite, and turn those telling paragraphs into show.

○ **Staging**

Look for...

- A character crossing a room.
- A character getting out of their car.
- Specifying that the left hand picked up a glass.
- Stating exactly where all the characters are standing/sitting/taking a breath.

Unless is it necessary to the plot that it's a five-step stroll from the main character's living room to the kitchen, cut it.

○ **The Placeholders**

If you've noted add more here or named your characters *NameLater*, find these placeholders and replace with the correct/more detail.

The Author Blind Spot Checklist

WHEN YOU'RE THE WRITER of a story, everything about it makes sense. And why wouldn't it? You're the one who's spent hours penning countless drafts.

The trouble with being the person who has worked on the story so intensely is that it can create an author blind spot. This is where you're too close to the work to see that things are confusing, missing, or not on the page as you intended.

No writer wants those type of issues messing up their story, and while it'll take the help of beta readers to spot any glaring problems, you can make it easier for them and you by running your manuscript through these checklist items first.

Confusing Mystery

Your story doesn't have to be a mystery to have a mysterious element to it. An event hinted at but not revealed right away can find a place in any genre. But, if your mysterious hints *don't* have a clear-cut answer or are too vague, you risk creating confusion rather than intrigue.

As the author who knows *both* the mystery and the outcome, you may not realize this. To fix it…

- Confirm that your hints are balanced with solid info.

That doesn't mean giving the answer straight away, especially if it's part of a later payoff, but ensuring your clues aren't murky. You don't want your reader feeling like they've missed something or are reading about an event they're only getting half the story of.

It's a fine line, but one you'll want to get right. A good way to tell if you've missed the mark is with beta feedback. If others are telling you they don't get something, listen to them and reassess.

Missing Character Motives

When you've been writing your characters for years, it's safe to say you know them better than anyone.

You've been through multiple drafts together, plot lines that didn't pan out, and rewrites that may have changed their history, backstory, name, and gender. Sometimes, this evolving relationship can lead to motives getting mixed up, switched, or left out completely.

As the author, *you* remember why your characters are doing what they're doing because you were with them for all of the drafts. But if you've forgotten that you cut a paragraph mentioning a motive three drafts ago, anyone who reads your latest will *not* know what's pushing your character.

If feedback tells you there's confusion about a character's motivation, and you can't understand why because you're sure it's in the draft, take another look. It's possible you removed something important, or things just aren't coming across the way you intended.

- Comb your draft, character by character, to confirm every motivation is clear.

It may be as simple as adding a line of dialogue, as complicated as going five drafts back and resurrecting a scene you cut, or it might require a totally new scene that has to be slotted in.

Do whatever it takes to ensure that your character motivations are present for anyone else who will read your book.

Subtle Settings

This is another one of those issues that crops up when you've fully immersed yourself in your fictional world.

The settings are very familiar to *you*. Or you feel you explained them in depth at the start of the story, and now you're blind to keeping the setting alive in the reader's mind in later chapters.

This isn't about describing a room in detail *every* time the character walks into it, but about reminding the reader where they are. They don't know the world like you do and will need something to ground them.

- Study the setting in each scene and make sure you've included enough info for readers to know where the characters are in that very moment.

It can be a paragraph of description or a simple reminder that the couch in the living room of your main character's house is lumpy as they sit down to watch TV.

Take off your author glasses and put on your reader glasses to make sure every scene has something that provides a description about where it's set, even if you feel like you've described it before.

Overwhelming Info

This is not the same as info-dumping. You aren't spending ten paragraphs cramming in backstory when a character is first introduced. This is about overwhelming the reader with *so much* info because, as the author, your blind spot is telling you it's all needed.

- Space out your info. Introduce your world's magic system as it crops up within different parts of the story, not with five pages as soon as the main character first discovers it.

I know it's hard to not explain your world-building genius as soon as you can, but overcoming this author blind spot will be appreciated by your readers.

While it might be a shock to realize that you've created problems in your manuscript, and that you couldn't see them, the good news is that they should be an easy fix. The kind that will ensure your story comes across as you always intended.

Related Checklists

The Settings Checklist
The Info-Dumping Checklist
The Character Motivation Checklist

The Author Blind Spot Checklist

☐ Confusing Mystery

If others tell you they don't get something, listen and reassess.

- Confirm that your hints are balanced with solid info.
- Ensure your clues aren't murky.

☐ Missing Character Motives

Make sure your character motivations are present and accounted for.

- Comb your draft by character to confirm that every motivation is clear.

It may be as simple as adding a line of dialogue, as complicated as going five drafts back and resurrecting a cut scene or it might require a totally new scene.

☐ Subtle Settings

With the settings so familiar, you could be blind about keeping them alive in the reader's mind.

- Study the setting in each scene and make sure you've included enough info for readers to know where the characters are in that very moment.

It can be a paragraph of description or a simple reminder that the couch in the living room of your main character's house is lumpy as they sit down to watch TV.

☐ Overwhelming Info

Don't give the reader too much info at once because, as the author, your blind spot is telling you it's *all* need to know.

- Space out your info, giving it as it crops up naturally, not with a five page info-dump as soon as anything happens.

The Review Draft Checklist

While your latest finished manuscript is off with beta readers or an editor, you'll most likely turn your attention to any other completed drafts.

Since it may have been a while between edits, getting them ready for the next stage and/or familiarizing yourself with the story again, will mostly likely require some work. Work that can be made easier by using this checklist to create a review plan.

Print the Manuscript

When you want to go over an manuscript, but don't want to spend that time editing constantly, print things out.

- Print your manuscript.

On the computer, it's too easy to tinker instead of just reading through what's there—which is a goal of this review.

Of course, if you're not a fan of printing, can't print, or you *can* trust yourself *not* to edit as you go, you can work off a screen.

Staple the Manuscript Into Chapters

Regardless of whether your printout is a small stack of A4 pages, or a mountain of reams, break that overwhelming pile into something smaller.

- Separate the manuscript into chapters.
- Staple each chapter together.

This will automatically give you smaller chunks to work on and you'll be able to break your review into daily or weekly goals, such as working through five chapters a day.

Decide on Two Focuses

While the primary goal of this review is to familiarize yourself with the story again, it's also a good chance to look for other things.

One advantage of reading an manuscript you may not have worked on/read in a while is that you've likely forgotten most of what you've written. This makes a read-through like this perfect for picking up typos and inconsistencies.

- Typos—they should jump out, so grab yourself a colored highlighter and mark them as you find them.

- Inconsistencies—look for a wrong character name or description, an object showing up in chapter twelve even though it was destroyed in chapter five, and the mention of an event that isn't anywhere else in the book. Give them a highlight too (in another color), and if need be, make an editing note in the margin.

If typos and inconsistencies aren't what you want to focus on, pick something else, just keep it to *two* editing items so this review is productive and efficient.

Add a Summary

On the blank back page of each chapter section…

- Jot down a summary of what happened. You can do this in bullet points, or as a timeline paragraph of each major event.

- Any better ideas for the story you had while reading.

- Any changes to make.

The change notes will help you later when you're editing, and the summary will help you with the next step.

Create an Outline

After reading through all your chapters and making a summary, create an outline of the whole manuscript.

- Go as light or as in-depth as you like.
- Note the most important events in each chapter so you can look at how the overall story is tracking.
- List where the scene took place.
- Note which character POV the scene is from.
- Other important details you feel should be included.

With your outline in place, it's time to plan.

Plan the Next Draft

Once you know how the story currently flows, plan the next draft.

With your outline as the guide...

- Look at what scenes need changing.
- What needs to be moved.
- What needs to be deleted.
- List which new event/scene needs to be added.
- Plan the changes to make and how you'll make them.
- Make notes for said changes in a notebook and highlight or tick each one as you achieve it.

Or form your own plan with whatever method works for *you*.

Set Yourself a Deadline

It's overwhelming to read a whole manuscript again, and hard to deal with all the fixes without freaking out.

If you're double-digits deep into your manuscript draft numbers, and the thought of extensive changes *yet again* only inspires you to procrastinate, set yourself a deadline.

- It could be for a set time, like a month, 3 months, or 1 year.
- Or set a commitment to work on your review for 1 hour every day until it's done.

Whichever option you choose, it'll ensure that you don't waste time or put things off for too long.

At the end of your review, you should have a good idea of your story, a bunch of typos and inconsistencies to fix, a summary of events, an outline, and a plan for what you're going to edit.

Done in a reasonable time-frame, you should be tackling your next draft ASAP and moving one step closer to making this reviewed manuscript your next finished book.

Related Checklists

The Reverse Outline Checklist
The Fresh Eyes Typo Hunting Checklist
The Final Draft Checklist

The Review Draft Checklist

○ **Print the Manuscript**
A physical copy will help you read what's there, but if you can't print, or you can trust yourself not to edit as you go, work off your screen.

○ **Staple the Manuscript Into Chapters**
Separate the manuscript into chapters, staple each chapter together, and work in smaller chunks to break your review into daily or weekly goals, such as working through five chapters a day.

○ **Decide on Two Focuses**
This review read-through is perfect for picking up typos and inconsistencies, so highlight both (in different colors) as you come across them.

- Typos.
- Inconsistencies, such as the wrong character names or descriptions, an object showing up in chapter twelve even though it was destroyed in chapter five, or the mention of an event that isn't anywhere else in the book.

If need be, make an editing note in the margin.

If typos and inconsistencies aren't what you want to focus on, feel free to pick something else, just keep it to two editing items so this review is productive and efficient.

○ **Add a Summary**
At the end of each chapter read...

- Jot down a summary of what happened in bullet points or a timeline paragraph of each major event.
- Any better ideas for the story.
- Any changes to make.

The Review Draft Checklist

◯ Create an Outline
Of the whole manuscript...

- Go as light or as in-depth as you like.
- Note the most important events in each chapter so you can look at how the overall story is tracking.
- List where the scene took place.
- Note which character POV the scene is from.
- Other important details you feel should be included.

◯ Plan the Next Draft
With your outline as the guide...

- Look at what scenes need changing.
- What needs to be moved.
- What needs to be deleted.
- List which new event/scene needs to be added.
- Plan the changes to make and how you'll make them.
- Make notes for said changes in a notebook and highlight or tick off each one as you achieve it.

◯ Set Yourself a Deadline
Make it for a specific length of time like a month, 3 months, or 1 year. Or set a commitment to work on your review for 1 hour every day until it's done.

The Edit Letter Checklist

When you reach the stage where your manuscript is nearly finished, you can't help but wonder what *still* needs to be done to create that final draft.

This part of the process can be overwhelming, especially after you've spent *so long* getting your novel to this point.

In the traditional publishing world, an agent or an editor would help you navigate this stage by writing an edit letter.

Such a tool is an excellent way to help you iron out any doubts, confusion, or errors left in the manuscript, and ensure your final draft is the best version of your manuscript that it can be.

For those not being traditionally published, or who aren't yet signed with an agent or editor, that initial edit letter can come from yourself.

The Ground Rules

For your edit letter, you'll want some distance.

- Write it in the third person, as if you're penning it to someone else.
- Be honest. *You* know the issues with your manuscript.
- Write down every little doubt, even that one about chapter three that you've been ignoring for the last two drafts.

Just as if you were giving feedback to someone else, give yourself the feedback that will be the most helpful.

What to Include

Now, for the actual letter contents itself, this should be based on what will work for *you*.

- Be as brief, or be as lengthy as you want.
- Write each change in detail or in general terms.
- Write everything from the first chapter to the last.
- And/or a general overview of the entire book.

We all write differently and will edit the same. Your edit letter should also suit your style and be in a structure that will work *for you*. You're the one who has to use it to shape your next draft, and if writing every single event in a ten-page edit letter allows you to do that, that's what you'll do.

The Good Parts

Go with what you did right and shower yourself with compliments!

- Bullet point everything you *love* about your manuscript.

The Improvements

Note down what could be…

- Improved.
- Which scenes are still weak.
- Anything that can be tweaked with some more editing/brainstorming.

The Bad Parts

This is where you'll note what isn't working and what needs to be fixed.

- Major problems.

- Characters that don't work.
- Confusing sections of plot.
- Character arcs that don't complete.
- Foreshadowing or clues that don't lead to anything.

Ignoring the villain having no motive may have gotten you through that last draft, but now it, and everything you know deep down isn't working, needs to be addressed.

The Nitty-Gritty

Pencil down the nitty-gritty of what you're willing to do for the next editing pass.

- What you'd like to edit.
- What you can edit.
- What you don't want to edit and why.
- What you're willing to compromise and fix, not remove.
- What can be removed.
- Solutions for backup fixes/changes.
- What you aren't willing to remove and why.

The Overview

This edit letter isn't just about fixing issues, it's also about understanding your story and the characters. Make room for an overview of the following...

Plot

- Write about what happens overall.

Characters

- Who they are? Summarize their arcs and relationships to one another.

Writing Style

Does the style you've written the novel in work?

- Is it consistent?
- Is there a certain chapter/scene that is the standard of how the entire novel should be written?

If so, make sure every chapter reads like it.

The Little Details

This section of the letter is for the little details that need attention...

- Include things like the eye color of each character.
- If an event is repeatedly mentioned.
- If the knife found at the murder scene was foreshadowed correctly.
- If the killer escaping through the building is a factually correct event.

This is where you'll make notes of the details that need to be double-checked, ironed out, and removed or corrected.

Direction

While telling another writer how to write/fix things (unless they have specifically asked you to) is a no-no, this edit letter is for yourself, and you need to tell yourself how to fix things.

- It's not helpful to say chapter three is boring; write why it's boring.
- Brainstorm how you'll fix any issues you've found.

Expectations

When noting down what needs to be revised, don't forget to include what you want the book to be. *Kick-Ass* and *Awesome*, as true as it might be, are too general.

- Go into specifics—such as if you want the reader to feel sorry for your villain, cry along with your main character, or swoon at the love story.

Note down those goals so you can ensure you've hit them.

If you want this book to be the one to land you an agent, a bestseller flag on Amazon, a publishing deal, or an award, put it in print. You're the only one reading this. Allow yourself to be open and dream big.

When you've completed *your* version of an edit letter, you should have a clear idea of your book. You should know what works, what doesn't, what needs to be removed, what still needs work, what you want the final version to be, and how to get there.

Related Checklists

The Little Details Checklist
The Review Draft Checklist

 The Edit Letter Checklist

○ **The Ground Rules**
Write it in the third person, be honest, be as brief or as lengthy as you want, and list each change in detail or in general terms.

○ **The Good Parts**
- Bullet point everything you love about your manuscript.

○ **The Improvements**
- List what could be improved.
- Which scenes are still weak.
- Anything that can be tweaked with some more editing/brainstorming.

○ **The Bad Parts**
- List major problems.
- Characters that don't work.
- Confusing sections of the plot.
- Character arcs that don't complete.
- Foreshadowing or clues that don't lead to anything.

○ **The Nitty-Gritty**
Note down...

- What you'd like to edit.
- What you can edit.
- What you don't want to edit and why.
- What you're willing to compromise and fix, not remove.
- What can be removed.
- Solutions for backup fixes/changes.
- What you aren't willing to remove and why.

✓ The Edit Letter Checklist

○ **The Plot**
Briefly note down what happens in the overall plot.

○ **The Characters**
- Make some notes about who they are.
- List their arcs.
- Write down their relationships with one another.

○ **The Writing Style**
- Does the style you've written the novel in work?
- Is it consistent?
- Make sure every chapter reads to the same standard.

○ **The Little Details**
Note down what needs to be double-checked, ironed out, removed or corrected, and include...

- The physical descriptions of each character.
- If an event is repeatedly mentioned.
- If everything is foreshadowed correctly.
- If events are factually correct.

○ **Direction**
Tell yourself how to fix things.

- It's not helpful to say chapter three is boring; write why it's boring.
- Brainstorm how you'll fix any issues you've found.

○ **Expectations**
List specifics—such as if you want the reader to feel sorry for your villain, cry along with your main character, or swoon at the love story.

Rewrites

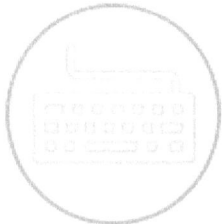

Rewriting can be a big job, but you can make the process easier with these two checklists. They will help you pinpoint what areas to work on if you feel like your manuscript isn't quite ready, but you're not sure what to fix, and some basic editing items to work through when you don't have time for a full edit.

The Something Is Missing Checklist

WHILE A BOOK MAY never be finished for the author, sometimes it's more than just being a perfectionist.

If you hear a little voice during a read-through, listen to it. Most likely, it's picking up on the things a reader will, like that cliffhanger line falling flat or that scene feeling rushed.

If you've listened and you're missing *something* but you're not sure what, the tips in this checklist should help you find what it is.

Starts

Opening lines make the first impression, and where your story starts impacts the rest of the plot. If something feels off, examine your starts.

- Make sure the story has started in the right place. An exciting incident helps draw readers in. Starting with your character going about their day is boring.

- Check to see if a scene starts where it needs to. This is not always about action, either. Sometimes dropping the reader in amongst things can disorientate and walking your scene back a few steps will help.

- Study the start of every sentence to make sure it's not a repeat of other opening sentences.

Settings/Descriptions

While you don't want to overwhelm the reader with boring setting details and descriptions that drone on about the design of the main character's coffee cup, you want to give your settings and descriptions some attention.

There is a fine balance. Too little attention and the world won't come across as a living place. Too much and the reader will zone out.

To get the right mix...

- Use clear, consistent details.

- Go for vivid words that will add the description in as few words as possible.

You want the readers to picture things, but not take four paragraphs to get there.

Motivation

Sometimes the missing element is why your characters are doing things. You might have made it clear why your main character needs to find a cursed book, but why does he do everything else he does while hunting it down?

If the reasons for motivation aren't there, you won't have well-rounded characters, which can contribute to that missing feeling.

- Check that it's clear on the page why your characters are acting the way they are.

It could make a world of difference to your manuscript.

Characters

As your drafts progressed, certain characters might not be important anymore, but as the author who created them, it's hard to see that. What can also be true is too many characters, two characters that could be combined into one, or a character that needs a bigger role.

In these cases, take a good look at each character in your story and decide if they can be cut, changed, or expanded.

As for the main characters of your book, if you think something is missing from them, double-check...

- Their backstory. Do the readers know enough about each character?
- Are they relatable?
- Perform a character edit for their specific POV, mannerisms, and dialogue. Each one should suit the individual character.

Internal Thoughts

Another suspect in the missing game is internal thoughts—either not enough or none at all.

The internal thoughts of your characters allow readers to get inside their heads. It's a great Deep POV tool, so if you haven't already implemented internal thoughts, and it would suit your genre and writing style, try adding them.

- Give the reader a close perspective of things through the eyes, thoughts, and feelings of the POV character.

It might just be what your story needs to take it to the next level.

If you're already incorporating internal thoughts, make sure you don't add too much or not enough. Balance is your friend and the key to filling what's missing.

World-Building

When you think of stories with great world-building, you know the author got it right. They're not lacking anything in the universe they've created.

If you're writing your first book, no one expects your world to be as fantastical or as strong as the books that set world-building standards, but if your book world is off, this is a great aspect to check.

- Refine how your story world works.

- Make sure world rules are set out.
- Confirm that magic systems aren't confusing.
- Double-check that how the society functions is clear (including diversity, religion, politics, gender, and race where/if relevant).

Pacing

Usually, the red flag of pacing is that a scene feels rushed. This can be down to missing internal thoughts, backstory, settings, descriptions, or anything else listed in this checklist, but sometimes it's simply down to pacing.

If the scene reads rushed, and you've included all the relevant details, study your pacing...

- Does the scene fly through explanations?
- Is there too little action?
- Have you tried to make things faster by writing quick action and clipped dialogue, but it's made the scene end prematurely?

On the flip side, maybe you've dragged things out?

- Is there too much action and dialogue?
- Have things slowed down because the main character stops to internally muse about something that happened five years ago? It might be relevant somewhere in the story, but not here amongst the action.
- Scrutinize the pacing of your scenes. There's a difference between rushed action and action that is rushing.

Important scenes that build character or reveal info also need balanced pacing so the characters and the readers can absorb what's happening (see *The Scene Sequel Checklist*).

If the pacing is off, you might just have found the missing element that's stopping your story from flowing.

Foreshadowing

Pulling off a good reveal isn't just down to the twist itself, but a combo of it and some plot sleight-of-hand.

Reveals work best when the reader suspects something is happening. They may be wrong or they may be right, but they need to know something is up. As the writer, you make this happen with foreshadowing.

If foreshadowing isn't part of your book, that might be what's making you doubt what's on the page.

- Check that your best book moments have been foreshadowed correctly.

This can take some practice to get right, but once you do, it's an awesome writing trick to master.

Ends

The final sentence of any book is just as important as the opening.

While the opening should draw the reader in, the end should resolve everything that's happened. If it's not, see if you've done the following...

- Verify you haven't rushed the big climax.
- Check that the last sentence of every scene is unique. You might have written similar endings during the months of writing and edits and not noticed.
- A final chapter sentence should either lead to the next scene in an exciting, cliffhanger-type way or resolve things in a satisfying way.

You want the last impression you leave on the reader to be as strong as possible. Get that right, and strike the best balance of the other items listed here, and your manuscript shouldn't be missing anything.

Related Checklists

The Book Openings Checklist
The Character Motivation Checklist
The Internal Thoughts Checklist
The World-Building Checklist
The Foreshadowing Checklist
The Chapter Endings Checklist

The Something Is Missing Checklist

○ **Starts**

If something feels off, examine your starts.

- Make sure the story has started in the right place. An exciting incident draws readers in. A character going about their day is boring.
- Check to see if a scene starts where it needs to and doesn't drop the reader in a disorientating situation.
- Study the start of every sentence to make sure it's not a repeat of other opening sentences.

○ **Settings/Descriptions**

Too little description and the world won't come across as a living place. Too much and the reader will zone out.

- Use clear, consistent details for setting/descriptions.
- Go for vivid words that will add the description in as few words as possible.
- You want readers to picture things, but not take four paragraphs to do it.

○ **Motivation**

Check that it's clear on the page why your characters are acting the way they are.

○ **Characters**

Take a good look at each character in your story and decide if they can be cut, changed, or expanded. For the main characters, double-check...

- Their backstory. Do the readers know enough about them?
- Are they relatable?
- Perform a character edit for their specific POV, mannerisms, and dialogue. Each one should suit the individual character.

The Something Is Missing Checklist

○ **Internal Thoughts**
Give the POV character's perspective using internal thoughts. If you already have, check the balance isn't too much or not enough.

○ **World-Building**
If your book world feels like it's missing something...

- Refine how your story world works.
- Make sure world rules are set out and systems aren't confusing.
- Confirm that how the society functions is clear.

○ **Pacing**
If the pacing is off, it might be the missing element of your story flow.

- Does the scene fly through explanations?
- Is there too little action?
- Has quick action and clipped dialogue made the scene too fast?

On the flip side, maybe you've dragged things out?

- Is there too much action and dialogue?
- Have things slowed because character's are internally musing at the wrong time?

○ **Foreshadowing**
If foreshadowing isn't part of your book, add it.

○ **Ends**
- Verify that you haven't rushed the big climax.
- Check that the last sentence of every scene is unique.
- A final chapter sentence should either have a cliffhanger-type lead or a satisfactory resolve.

The Bare Minimum Checklist

While checklists are a great way to whip your manuscript into shape, the thought of running through a vast set of tasks when you've just completed one can be overwhelming.

You want to ensure your manuscript is the best it can be, but you're also *very tired* of looking at every single sentence. The good news is that there's a checklist you can try.

For these checklist items, you'll be looking at the *bare minimum* of book elements to fix, allowing you to make changes to your manuscript, just not every single change at once. This makes it perfect for having a productive break after writing/editing, or to use when you have a tight deadline and can't complete a full checklist.

Book Based Spellings

While a spell check should have already highlighted errors in your manuscript, there are things that slip past, and it's usually the spellings unique to your book.

Use your *find/search* function to double-check the following for the correct spelling of...

Character Names

Regardless of whether you came up with your character's name by jumbling random letters together or going with the top three baby monikers of 2013, every name should be double-checked for spelling.

I know this from experience. In my series, *Blackbirch*, there's a character named *Kallie*, and no matter how many times I've typed her name across countless drafts, there is always at least one spelling where I have missed an l, making it *Kalie*.

That alternate spelling isn't picked up by my spell checker either, so I always do a manual check for her name, the misspelling, and the other character names and possible misspellings during a pass.

This way, I'll pick up any errors my fingers have mistyped and my read-this-a-million-times eyes have glossed over.

Places

Check for consistency regarding the places named in your manuscript that are unique to it or true to life. For example, if your main character works at Slinky's Pizzeria, make sure it's spelled and capitalized the same in every instance.

Use your *find/search* function to double-check the correct spelling and capitalization of...

- Town names.
- Countries.
- School names.
- Businesses.
- Workplaces.
- Any other place relevant/made up for your book world.

Correct Basic Punctuation

Even though this checklist search will take time, it still sticks to a minimum number of punctuations to keep the process as simple as possible.

Sentences

Find/search **? . !** and check that...

- The question mark (**?**) is at the end of anything that ends in a question.

- The full stop/period (**.**) is at the end of every sentence.

- That exclamation marks (**!**) aren't overused (if 1,000 show up, your writing style is way too excited!).

Dialogue

Find/search **."** and **,"** and check that...

- Action in dialogue is followed by a full stop/period—"Don't do that**.**" Carla **grabbed** her phone from Jenny's hand.

- Speech in dialogue is followed by a comma—"Don't do that**,**" Carla **said**.

Numbers

If a character checks the time, looks up a street address, or lists a date, there are numbers in your manuscript and it's important to check that they're written correctly and are consistent across the book.

Find/search...

Time

- Spelled out: Ten **o'clock** in the morning.

- Numerical: 10 **a.m.**

Numbers

- Spelled out: **One hundred**.

- Numerical: **100**.

Your Top Three Overused Words

As writers, we all have our own little touches that we bring to our work. That includes overusing favorite words or phrases.

It could be your affinity for the word affinity. You may not be able to write a scene where a character doesn't use their fingertips. Or your worst writer trait is overusing the term as if (she reached for him *as if* he was real. He fastened the seatbelt *as if* it was a lifeline keeping him tethered to the world).

- Make a list of your top three overused words/phrases (*you* know what they are) and engage that *find/search* function to either rewrite or delete them to an acceptable level.

Why top three? That's to keep to the bare minimum theme of this checklist. If you have over three, make a note to do the others when you have more time/are ready for a deeper editing dive.

Related Checklists

The Proofreading Checklist
The Fresh Eyes Typo Hunting Checklist

The Bare Minimum Checklist

○ Book Based Spellings

Use your *find/search* function to check the correct spelling and capitalization of...

- Character names.
- Places.
- Town names.
- Countries.
- School names.
- Businesses.
- Workplaces.
- Any other place relevant/made up for your book world.

○ Correct Basic Punctuation

Stick to checking a minimum number of punctuations to keep the process as simple as possible.

Sentences—*find/search* **?** . **!** and check that...

- The question mark (**?**) is at the end of anything that ends in a question.
- The full stop/period (.) is at the end of every sentence.
- That exclamation marks (**!**) aren't overused.

Dialogue—*find/search* **."** and **,"** and check that...

- Action in dialogue is followed by a full stop/period—"Don't do that**.**" Carla **grabbed** her phone from Jenny's hand.
- Speech in dialogue is followed by a comma—"Don't do that**,**" Carla **said**.

The Bare Minimum Checklist

○ **Numbers**
If a character checks the time, looks up a street address, or lists a date, there are numbers to check for correct and consistent use.

Time—*find/search*...
- Spelled out: **Ten o'clock in the morning.**
- Numerical: **10 a.m.**

Numbers—*find/search*...
- Spelled out: **One hundred.**
- Numerical: **100.**

○ **Your Top Three Overused Words**
Make a list of your top three overused words/phrases and use *find/search* to either rewrite or delete them to an acceptable level.

Proofing

To ensure your manuscript is as error free as possible, these checklists will allow you to hunt down typos while looking at your work with fresh eyes, and implement a proofreading plan that will help you revise your research, grammar, and other basic elements.

The Proofreading Checklist

PROOFREADING MAY BE THAT last thing you feel like doing after completing *yet another* editing pass of your manuscript, but if you're up to this stage, you are *so close* to the end.

Make revising your draft as easy as possible by breaking it down into tangible steps with the help of this checklist.

Make a List

Before you proofread, create a list of what you want to tackle; such as...

- Spelling.
- Grammar.
- Punctuation.
- Physical character descriptions (eye color, hair color, tall, short, etc.).
- Settings/Locations.
- Dialogue.
- Specifics for *your* book.

Make a basic list of common proofing goals (like those above), as well as a list of things to check that are specific to *your* book.

No one knows better than you which words or phrases you repeat, or that Timmy fell down the well in chapter three so he can't be at school in chapter four. A list that helps you narrow down what to look for will be a big help as you make your way through your edits.

Concentrate on One Task at a Time

Success is not about speed, as any writer playing the waiting game with a publisher will tell you. The same goes for proofreading.

If you try to speed up the process and revise dialogue while hunting typos, checking commas, ensuring that your main character's eye color doesn't change, and that the abandoned house they revisit in the final chapter is still located in the same section of town (unless it's a mysterious, traveling abandoned house), then checking *everything at once* is only going to result in mistakes.

- Concentrate on only *one* proofreading task at a time.

It will take longer and you will *hate* having to read your manuscript again when you reach the low end of your list, but it's the best way to pick up errors.

Utilize All the Help You Can

We're in a technologically advanced age where help with grammar and spelling is just a click away. Run those programs and let them pick up the errors that your tired, mere mortal eyes can't. Just don't rely on those programs to pick up everything or to choose the right word. After all, "dessert" is the correct (and yummy) spelling according to your computer spell check, but not what you intended when you left your protagonist "wandering the desolate, sand-covered desert."

- Have a thesaurus and dictionary within reach or bookmarked for easy access.

- Run a spell check program.

- Use a grammar check program.

- Use apps that will read your work aloud to you.

Double Check Your Research and Facts

You might have made sure that everything was correct when you started writing your first draft, but now it's been two years and you've aged twenty.

- Do one more check on your research and facts, especially for technology or world circumstances that may have changed.

By allocating at least *one* proofreading pass as a double check for your research, you'll ensure that all of your facts are still relevant, and/or get the chance to update the ones that aren't.

Mix It Up

Devote one proofreading pass to mixing up the way you read the manuscript.

- Read your book backward by starting from the last chapter and working your way to the first.

- Check chapters out of order.

- If you have alternating POV chapters, such as the main character and side character #1, list each chapter by each character and read your way through, concentrating on just the main character chapters for one pass, and then side character #1 on the second pass.

This should find any lingering problems—which then leaves you with only one hundred more proofreading passes to go!

Related Checklists

The Review Draft Checklist
The Bare Minimum Checklist

The Proofreading Checklist

○ **Make a List**
Create a list of what you want to tackle, such as...

- Spelling.
- Grammar.
- Punctuation.
- Physical character descriptions (eye color, hair color, tall, short, etc.).
- Settings/Locations.
- Dialogue.
- Specifics for your book.

○ **Concentrate on One Task at a Time**
It will take longer, but it's the best way to pick up errors.

○ **Utilize All the Help You Can**
Use technology and modern help by...

- Having a thesaurus and dictionary in reach or digitally bookmarked.
- Running a spell and grammar check program.
- Using apps that will read your work aloud to you.

○ **Double Check Your Research and Facts**
Do one more check, especially for changing tech or world circumstances.

○ **Mix It Up**
Devote one proofreading pass to mixing up your read through.

- Read your book backward.
- Check chapters out of order.
- If you have alternating POV chapters, such as the main character and a side character, read the main character's chapters for one pass, and then the side character's chapters on another.

The Fresh Eyes Typo Hunting Checklist

WHILE BEING ABLE TO *Google* the answer to any grammatical question is a modern godsend for writers, the one technological advance I'm sure most of us would love is the ability to see our work with fresh eyes and to spot all typos.

Short of a future app that makes it possible, or an amnesic accident, reading something that you've read a million times will limit your ability to proofread, and we all know typos aren't just wrong keystrokes or the ~~write~~ right word with the wrong spelling. They're tricksters—convincing your eyes that what they're reading is what your brain expects.

But where there's a will, there's a way. It *is* possible to turn yourself into a typo hunter who sees your words with fresh eyes—and your weapon of choice is this checklist.

Change the Font

Simple yet effective, changing the font for your manuscript mixes it up in your brain. Different colors can't hurt either, just don't spend all day switching between *Helvetica* and *Comic Sans* and forget to actually do some proofreading.

- Change your manuscript font.
- Change the color of the text.

It should be enough to help your eyes see your work in a fresh new way.

Print on Paper

This old-school tip not only gives your eyes a rest from staring at a screen all day, but seeing your words on paper also carries the bonus of making it easier to spot typos.

- Print out your manuscript and read your words from the printed page.

Have a Program Read It Out Loud

The future is here, at least in terms of apps that will read your work to you. Google *text-to-speech* and find a program that will read your words out loud, or into your headphones if you want to be discreet.

- Use a *text-to-speech* app or the *read aloud* feature of your writing program.

It's an excellent way to pick up issues of word flow or awkward paragraphs you might not find when relying on just your eyes.

Borrow Someone Else's Eyes

No, we still aren't there with technology yet, but you can give your manuscript to someone else to read.

- Ask a friend, family member, beta reader, or trusted member of the writing community to read your manuscript for you.

A different set of eyes is often the best way to find problem prose, and that doesn't just include typos. Another set of eyes is another brain processing your work, one who thinks differently to you and reads differently and can give you another opinion on what isn't working and pick up any issues.

Read It Differently

Add your manuscript to your Kindle, iPad, or phone. Sit outside if the weather is nice, or go to a café and order yourself some writer fuel and read while surrounded by the world.

- Read your manuscript in a different place from where you wrote it.

Anything that is different to the environment you're usually in when writing will give your senses a shake-up and help you see your manuscript in a different light.

As for trying to spot typos, while reading your manuscript is the easiest way to do that, because typos rely on your brain to sort the words into their familiar order, it can be just as easy to miss the misspellings.

- Try reading your manuscript in reverse sequence, starting at the last chapter and reading your way back to the first chapter.

This will pull one over on the part of your brain that knows the order the words are supposed to be in, helping you catch those typos.

Work in Sections

Sometimes even just the idea of having to read 80,000 words *yet again* is enough for your brain to count itself out before you even start.

If you want its help to track down any manuscript mistakes and typos...

- Break the task into sections.

- Read just one page and then take a break.

- Go scene-by-scene, or chapter-by-chapter.

- One trick I use is to copy 500 words of the manuscript into a different program or document, read/check that, and then move to the next 500 words.

Working in sections might seem like a slow way to work, but it helps you focus on the task at hand and not the 50,000 other words you've *still* got to go.

Go Out on a High(light)

If you've worked through every other tip and are still finding issues, or you want to be as thorough as possible, this extreme trick requires color.

- Get your hands on a colored highlighter.
- Print out your manuscript.
- As you read, highlight every word.

That's right. *Every. Single. Word.*

This kind of pass isn't about reading your story (which at this point you should be reciting from memory), it's about concentrating on each individual word and making sure it's correct. If an error or typo gets past this check, they are simply a part of your manuscript now and you should adjust your life accordingly.

Leave It Alone

Obviously, the best way to get truly fresh eyes is to have some time away from your work. That way, your brain gets the chance to forget most of what is written.

- Put your manuscript away for a set length of time before reading it again.

How long you leave your manuscript alone is a personal preference. Some writers insist that placing it in a drawer for a year is the best way to see your work with fresh eyes. If you can't do that, leave it for a month, a week, or even one day if you're really up against a deadline.

Basically, any time away gives you fresh eyes and a sixth sense for typos—or at least it will until technology catches up.

Related Checklists

The Proofreading Checklist

The Fresh Eyes Typo Hunting Checklist

○ **Change the Font**
Simple yet effective, changing the font and the text color for your manuscript mixes it up in your brain.

○ **Print On Paper**
Read your manuscript as a physical copy.

○ **Have a Program Read It Out Loud**
Find a *text-to-speech* program that will read your words to you.

○ **Borrow Someone Else's Eyes**
Ask a friend, family member, beta reader, or member of the writing community to read your manuscript to help find problems.

○ **Read It Differently**
Add your manuscript to your Kindle, iPad or phone and read it in a different place from where you wrote it. You can also start from the last chapter and read your way back through to the first.

○ **Work in Sections**
Read one page and then take a break. Go scene-by-scene, or chapter-by-chapter. Copy 500 words into a different document, check that, then the next 500 words.

○ **Go Out on a High(light)**
Print your manuscript and highlight every word as you read.

○ **Leave It Alone**
Put your manuscript away for a set length of time before reading it again. That way your brain gets the chance to forget the majority of what's written.

Editing Elements

The final checklists are not only some of the best, but they will whip your manuscript into shape by removing the words that clutter your sentences, help you perfect your dialogue and staging, allow you to get the little details right, make your writing active, and nail your chapters.

The Delete Checklist

WORDS. YOU CAN'T BE a writer without them. We use them to convey our thoughts and feelings and to create worlds and the characters that live in them. Words give us our voice, but they can also muddle it.

Just because you can write using all the words doesn't mean ~~that~~ you should.

Being too wordy can ~~actually~~ be a bad thing. It weakens sentences and takes the impact out of our paragraphs. This potentially stops something good from being great.

By removing unnecessary words, you're left with strong, clear prose.

But ~~some of~~ these words add depth and character, you might argue. *Yes*, they do. In the right sentence, ~~in~~ the right paragraph, at the right point in the story. Any other time, it's ~~likely to be~~ cluttering ~~up~~ your sentences.

To help you declutter, let me introduce you to *The Delete Checklist*.

Before you start, keep in mind that this isn't a complete checklist. Just as we all have our own personal *Repeats* list, you may wish to remove some words or add ~~in~~ others. What this checklist will do is give you and your *find/search* function a place to start.

The Rules:

Please remember that *not* every instance needs to be deleted. Use this check to take a close look at *how* you are using the word:

- If it makes sense **without it, cut it.**

- If it's **needed** for clarity/depth/etc., **keep it**.

For those wondering if you'll have any words left after going through *The Delete Checklist* found at the end of these tips, keep the following in mind...

Example:

Jenny knelt **down** to get the streamer and threw it in the bin. "Carla, when are you going to take these **down**?"

Not only is adding **down** twice in one sentence bad writing, it's the perfect example of why you should have a delete checklist.

Down is not needed in the first instance. We can assume Jenny knelt down because there is no other way to kneel. Asking Carla when she's going to take the streamers down, however, is necessary...

Example:

Jenny knelt to get the streamer and threw it in the bin. "Carla, when are you going to take these **down**?"

By deleting the first instance of down and keeping the second, the sentence is neater and still makes sense, and that is what a delete checklist will help you do.

Related Checklists

The Weak Word Checklist
The Reduce a Big Word Count Checklist

The Delete Checklist

IF IT MAKES SENSE WITHOUT IT, *CUT IT*.
IF IT'S NEEDED FOR CLARITY/DEPTH/ETC, *KEEP IT*.

Use Your *find/search* function to scour your manuscript for the following words, and remember that not every instance needs to be deleted.

○ Actually	○ I believe	○ Saw
○ Always	○ In order to	○ Seemed
○ Am	○ Inhale	○ Seems
○ Are	○ Is	○ Shrug
○ Around	○ Just	○ Shrugged
○ Asked	○ Kind of	○ So
○ Back	○ Like	○ Somehow
○ Basically	○ Literally	○ Somewhat
○ Began	○ May	○ Sort of
○ Begin	○ Maybe	○ Specific
○ Begun	○ Might	○ Start
○ Being	○ Nod	○ Started
○ Breath	○ Nodded	○ Such
○ Breathe	○ Noticed	○ Suddenly
○ But	○ Particular	○ That
○ Certainly	○ Ponder	○ Then
○ Completely	○ Possibly	○ Thing
○ Could	○ Probably	○ Think
○ Definitely	○ Quite	○ Thought
○ Down	○ Rather	○ Totally
○ Exhale	○ Reach	○ Type of
○ Extremely	○ Reached	○ Understand
○ Feel	○ Realize/Realise	○ Up
○ Felt	○ Realized/Realised	○ Very
○ Generally	○ Really	○ Virtually
○ Got		○ Was
○ Had		○ Were
○ Heard		○ Wonder

The Weak Word Checklist

Not all words are created equal, and as a writer, you can devote many hours to finding the perfect one.

While playing with word choice and rewriting sentences until you get them *just* right can help capture what you're trying to invoke, a weak word can do the opposite.

But how do you know which exact words will pull the strength from your sentences? That's a skill you'll learn to develop as you grow as a writer. In the meantime, the following checklist is a good place to start.

The Rules

Use your *find/search* function to scour your manuscript for the words listed in the checklist at the end of these tips.

- If your sentence **makes sense without** the weak word, **delete it.**
- If the weak word adds **clarity, keep it.**
- If deleting the weak word makes the sentence **better but confusing**, **delete** the **word** and **rewrite** the **sentence**.

Feel free to add or remove any words to suit your style and voice. I've used this checklist myself and it really tightened my sentences.

Examples: (*Taken from Blackbirch: The Beginning*)

Deleting a Weak Word for a Stronger Sentence:

Before: Eve spoke, cutting Sarah off before she could even **think** about opening her mouth.

After: Eve spoke, cutting Sarah off before she could open her mouth.

Deleting a Weak Word/s and Rewriting the Sentence:

Before: Sarah's ballet flat kicked something in the dark. Her first **thought** was a box, but as soon as she turned on the light, she **saw** Josh collapsed on the floor, his head **right** near the tip of her black shoe.

After: Sarah's ballet flat kicked something in the dark. *A box?* As soon as she turned on the light, she found Josh collapsed on the floor, his head near the tip of her black shoe.

As you can see, removing the weak words improved the sentences. Try it in your own manuscript, and happy weak word hunting!

Related Checklists

The Delete Checklist
The Early Draft Cuts Checklist

The Weak Word Checklist

IF YOUR SENTENCE MAKES SENSE WITHOUT THE WEAK WORD—*DELETE IT*

IF THE WEAK WORD ADDS CLARITY—*KEEP IT*

IF DELETING THE WEAK WORD MAKES THE SENTENCE BETTER BUT CONFUSING—*DELETE THE WORD AND REWRITE THE SENTENCE*

Use Your *find/search* function to scour your manuscript for the following words, and remember that not every instance needs to be deleted.

- ○ Actually
- ○ Always
- ○ Back
- ○ Basically
- ○ Being
- ○ But
- ○ Certainly
- ○ Completely
- ○ Could
- ○ Definitely
- ○ Extremely
- ○ Feel
- ○ Felt
- ○ Generally
- ○ Got
- ○ Had
- ○ Heard
- ○ Just
- ○ Kind of
- ○ Like
- ○ Literally
- ○ May
- ○ Maybe
- ○ Might
- ○ Particular
- ○ Ponder
- ○ Possibly
- ○ Probably
- ○ Quite
- ○ Rather
- ○ Realize / Realise
- ○ Realized / Realised
- ○ Really
- ○ Right
- ○ Saw
- ○ Seemed
- ○ Seems
- ○ So
- ○ Somehow
- ○ Somewhat
- ○ Sort of
- ○ Specific
- ○ Start
- ○ Started
- ○ Such
- ○ Suddenly
- ○ That
- ○ Then
- ○ Thing
- ○ Think
- ○ Thought
- ○ Totally
- ○ Type of
- ○ Very
- ○ Virtually
- ○ Wonder

The Active Checklist

One well-known piece of writing advice is to keep your prose active, but when you're first starting out, you have *no idea* what words are making your prose non-active.

You're just using the words that sound right, and it's not until you see the difference creating an active voice makes to your story that you understand why it's a tried-and-true recommendation.

Examples: *(Taken from Blackbirch: The Beginning)*

Non-Active: Sarah's fingers fumbled in her skirt pocket, **trying** to reach for her cell phone.

Active: Sarah's fingers fumbled in her skirt pocket for her cell phone.

Non-Active: The fire at the entrance **had** reached one of the glass doors and **was** turning it black.

Active: The fire at the entrance reached one of the glass doors, turning it black.

Do you see the difference removing only a few words can make? Do you want to do the same for your own sentences? If your answer is *yes*, this checklist is your ticket.

The Rules

Use your *find/search* function to dig through your manuscript for the words listed in the following checklist.

Related Checklists

The Weak Word Checklist
The Delete Checklist

The Active Checklist

IF YOUR SENTENCE MAKES SENSE WITHOUT THE WORD—*DELETE IT*

IF THE WORD ADDS CLARITY—*KEEP IT*

IF DELETING THE WORD MAKES THE SENTENCE CONFUSING
—*REWRITE THE SENTENCE*

Use Your *find/search* function to scour your manuscript for the following words/phrases, and remember that not every instance needs to be deleted.

○ Appeared	○ Noticed	**Active Phrases**
○ Began	○ Possibly	○ Could feel
○ Begin	○ Prayed	○ Could hear
○ Begun	○ Probably	○ Could see
○ Believed	○ Realize / Realise	○ Could smell
○ Considered	○ Realized / Realized	○ Had been
○ Could	○ Saw	○ Has been
○ Decided	○ Seemed	○ Have been
○ Did	○ Seems	○ The feel of
○ Does	○ Smelled	○ The smell of
○ Feel	○ Start	○ The sound of
○ Felt	○ Started	○ Tried to
○ Had	○ Thought	
○ Has	○ Tried	
○ Have	○ Trying	
○ Heard	○ Was	
○ Hoped	○ Watched	
○ Knew	○ Understand	
○ Looked	○ Were	
○ Maybe	○ Wondered	
○ Might		

The Stage Direction Checklist

WE ALL HAVE A writing habits that are hard to break no matter how much we improve as a writer. For many wordsmiths, myself included, stage directing is one of those habits.

If you're a writer who can't help but describe everything a character sees in unnecessary detail and every physical move beyond what's needed, this checklist will help flag the words that indicate stage directing so you can weed it out.

The reason you want to keep stage direction to a minimum is to keep the action going, up the tension, move the plot forward, and to use your words to reveal things about your character, not waste them describing how they crossed from one side of the room to the other.

To get started, let's look at some stage direction with our trusty Example Characters, Jenny and Carla.

All the stage direction words are in **bold**.

Example:

With Stage Direction:
Jenny **entered** the room by **reaching** for the heavy door and **pushing** on its handle.
She **glanced** at the faces, **looking** for Carla. When she saw her, she **walked** to the table and stood alongside it.
"Thought you could hide from me, huh?"
Carla **turned**. "Jenny, what are you doing here?"
Jenny **lifted** her purse, **pulling** her phone out and waving it in Carla's face. "You went there. I have pictures!"

"What? Are you stalking me now?" Carla rolled her eyes.
"Don't lie about it!" Jenny waved the phone around, shoving it back in Carla's face.
Carla **grabbed** for it, but Jenny held it back. "You promised you wouldn't go to the police."

Without Stage Direction:

Jenny bustled into the room, scanning the faces for Carla. *There she is.* "Thought you could hide from me, huh?"
Carla stared at her from the other side of the table. "Jenny, what are you doing here?"
Jenny fished her phone from her purse, waving it in Carla's face. "You went there. I have pictures!"
"What? Are you stalking me now?" Carla rolled her eyes.
"Don't lie about it!"
Carla grabbed for the phone, but Jenny held it back. "You promised you wouldn't go to the police."

By cutting out most of the stage directing words, the scene is tighter and faster-paced, which suits the feel.

The idea that Jenny has come into a crowded room looking for Carla and finds her at a table still comes across, but it doesn't take as long to get to that conclusion.

It's also still obvious that Jenny takes her phone out of her purse, you just don't get a step-by-step account anymore. Removing the staging words around the dialogue also makes it snappier, and "grabbed" is kept because it works.

Eliminating the staging has made for a quicker, more interesting read, and the swaps are easy to achieve, once you know what words to flag and check.

Another staging red flag is describing a room in such a way your reader might wonder if your day job is to sell furniture.

Example:

Too Much Furniture Description:

The hotel room was small and neat, with a single bed covered in a thick quilt taking up most of the space. Jenny glanced around at its bare beige walls before flopping on the end of the bed and staring up at the rusted ceiling fan above her.

Stealthy Furniture Description:
Jenny flopped onto the end of the bed, throwing her bag down. It bumped against the beige wall, leaving a scuff mark that gave it some color. She stretched back onto the quilt, her calloused hands finding warmth and comfort in its thickness. The ceiling fan above her was the messiest feature of the room, bent at an odd angle and dotted with rust. *I won't be switching you on.* It would be just her luck for it to come loose and crush her in her sleep.

The first example might give the reader an idea of the room, but it doesn't tell them anything about Jenny.

With the staging rewritten in the second example, it still comes across that the hotel room is small and neat, with a single bed, boring walls, and a rusted ceiling fan, but we also learn about Jenny. She's a physical worker, down on her luck, with calloused hands, looking for warmth and comfort. By rewriting the staging and having her interact with what's around her instead of just stating it, the reader learns about the character and is painted a picture of the scene instead of reading a list of hotel furniture.

Does this mean you should never describe furniture or give the reader an idea of where a character is standing in a scene? *Of course not.* As with all writing tricks, you need to learn how to balance the staging.

If you're unsure what staging to keep or cut, ask yourself if the action/direction is needed or if you're just stating what the reader can work out for themselves. Have some trust they'll *get* that a character crosses from one side of the room to another without spelling it out.

Use this knowledge and checklist to scour your own sentences and cut the stage directing habit once and for all.

The Rules:

Look at each instance of the words featured in the following checklist and see if you can eliminate, rewrite or swap the word out for an action beat.

Related Checklists

The Tension Checklist
The Action Beats Checklist
The Active Checklist

The Stage Direction Checklist

LOOK AT EACH INSTANCE AND SEE IF YOU CAN *ELIMINATE, REWRITE* OR *SWAP THE WORD OUT FOR AN ACTION BEAT.*

Use Your *find/search* function to scour your manuscript for the following words, and remember that not every instance needs to be deleted/changed.

- Entered
- Exited
- Glance
- Glancing
- Glanced
- Grab
- Grabbing
- Grabbed
- Lifted
- Look
- Looked
- Looking
- Pull
- Pulling
- Pulled
- Pushing
- Push
- Pushed
- Reach
- Reaching
- Reached
- Tipped
- Turn
- Turning
- Turned
- Walking
- Walk
- Walked

The Dialogue Checklist

WHILE IT'S UP TO you to perfect your dialogue, and *The Dialogue Tips Checklist* can help you do that, to ensure you have the rules and punctuation of dialogue correct, run through *this* checklist.

The Rules

Use your *find/search* function to find every quote mark (" or '), and when they're highlighted in your document, check...

Spelled Out Emotions

Even though there's nothing wrong with occasionally telling emotions, if you're doing it throughout your *whole* manuscript, use this editing pass to find all that *telling* and convert some to *showing*.

Examples:

Telling: "Get out!" Jenny **shouted angrily**.

Showing: "Get out!" Jenny **shook her fists, her cheeks flushing red**.

Character Names

Look at your usage of character names. Have you used them too much? Not enough?

If it's *not* clear who's speaking, pair character names with your dialogue tags. If it *is* clear, consider removing names to tighten your prose and word count.

Examples:

Character Names:
"What time are we leaving tonight?" **Jenny** asked.
"I told him we'd be there at nine," **Carla** said.

Names Removed:
Jenny's gaze followed Carla as she took the seat opposite her. "What time are we leaving tonight?"
"I told him we'd be there at nine."

Dialogue Tags

If you've heard the theory that *said* is the perfect dialogue tag because readers overlook it, there's also a theory about mixing things up with other tags like *screamed* and *demanded*.

- Decide what's best for your story and use this editing pass to study each tag for the right balance.

Action Beats

Another option for mixing up your dialogue tags is not using one at all.

As you're checking your dialogue...

- See if it's suitable to end a line with an action beat instead.

- Or make sure you have a good ratio of actions beats to dialogue tags.

Examples:

Dialogue Tag: "I'm just joking," Carla **said**.

Action Beat: "I'm just joking." Carla **fiddled with the ends of her hair, tucking a strand behind her ear**.

Punctuation

When combining punctuation and grammar with your dialogue, the key is consistency and remembering some basics.

- If you're using **single (')** or **double (")** quotation marks, stick with the **one** option throughout your manuscript.

- **Dialogue** goes **inside the quote marks**.

- Check that there's **no missing punctuation** in your dialogue. It's easy to forget a comma, full stop/period, question mark, or exclamation point when you're typing furiously.

- If your dialogue is followed by a **speaking tag** like *said, whispered, hissed*, punctuate it with a **comma**.

- If it's followed by an **action** like *moved, stood, closed the door*, use a **full stop/period**.

- Any **subject** (he, she, they) *after* a punctuation mark in dialogue should be in **lowercase**, not uppercase.

Examples:

Missing Punctuation: "I know you're lyin**g**" Jenny shouted (should be a **,** between **g** and **"**).

Comma for Speaking Tag: "I know you're lying," **Jenny shouted**.

Full Stop/Period for Action Tag: "I know you're lying." **Jenny smashed the vase.**

Lowercase Subject: "Are you lying?" she asked.

Related Checklists

The Dialogue Tips Checklist
The Show Don't Tell Checklist
The Action Beats Checklist

The Dialogue Checklist

◯ **Use Your Find/Search Function To**
Find every quote mark (" or '), and when they're highlighted in your document, check...

◯ **Spelled Out Emotions**
Find any telling and convert some of it to showing to create a better balance for your dialogue.

◯ **Character Names**
Balance using or dropping them. If it's not clear who's speaking, add names to your dialogue tags. If it is clear, remove names to tighten things.

◯ **Dialogue Tags**
Decide the variety of dialogue tags you want to use and get the right balance.

◯ **Action Beats**
Check if it's more suitable to end a line with an action beat instead of dialogue, or make sure you have a good ratio of action beats to dialogue tags.

◯ **Punctuation**
Keep it consistent and remember the basics.

- Decide on either single (') or double (") quotation marks.
- Dialogue goes inside quote marks.
- Check that there's no missing punctuation in your dialogue.
- Use a comma when dialogue has a tag (said, whispered, shouted).
- Use a full stop/period when dialogue has an action (smiled, laughed).
- Any subject (he, she, they) *after* a punctuation mark in dialogue should be in lowercase not uppercase.

The Chapter Checklist

HAVE YOU EVER BEEN caught in an endless editing loop, completing spell checks, eliminating repeats, and ensuring all the characters aren't grinning too much?

If the answer is yes, I'm sure you're more than ready to move to the next step. But before you do, there is one more check, something beyond ensuring you haven't overused *that* or double-checked that every character isn't constantly nodding.

Enter *The Chapter Checklist!*

For this checklist, we're going to take on each chapter, page by page.

To start, print out your manuscript and staple each individual chapter together to work on using highlighters, Post-its for notes, and a red/colored pen for corrections. Or you can work from your screen using digital highlighters and note-taking features in your preferred writing program.

The key is to *concentrate* on *one chapter* at a time, so it's not overwhelming, and to remember that this *isn't* the time to edit or rewrite.

Use a critical eye to look at what each chapter contains and note down what changes to make during your next edit.

The Length

Some writers work to specific word counts for a chapter, others write it as long as it needs to be.

Whatever method you use, take the opportunity now to…

- Look at your chapter lengths and see if any need to be adjusted.

- If a chapter is too long, cut it down or split it up.
- If it's too short, brainstorm what you can add to make it longer, i.e., more detailed descriptions, an extra scene, etc.

These tasks can then be completed in your next editing pass.

The Openings and Endings

Or, as I also like to call it, the tops and tails of each chapter. Here we will...

- Check the opening sentence/paragraph.
- Look at the closing sentence/paragraph.

These are important to check because it's very easy to open a scene similarly when you've been penning a book over months or years.

- Checking the first sentence/paragraph of every chapter one after the other allows you to see if you've made this mistake.
- As for the endings, try to close each scene with a hook, cliffhanger, or closure.

Using this checklist to scrutinize each last sentence will ensure you're doing just that.

The Balance

Of scene/sequels and unanswered questions.

One of my favorite writing methods is using scenes and sequels within a chapter. If you're not familiar with it, a scene is when you have an event, like an exciting incident, and the sequel is dealing with the consequences of that incident (for tips on writing a scene sequel, see *The Scene Sequel Checklist*).

For this checklist item...

- Read each scene in your chapter.

- Work out if it's a scene or sequel (if you don't know already).

- Ensure there's a balance of both.

Another thing to balance is your unanswered questions. Every unanswered question needs an answer in your story (unless it's a hook for the next book in the series).

- Use your chapter read to highlight any unanswered question so you know it's there and can look for the answer in other chapters.

If you find you don't have a good balance of unanswered questions, or there are ones that need answers in this book but you haven't done it yet (it happens), make a note to add it to your next draft to-do list.

The Timeline

Looking at each chapter closely gives you the perfect chance to note down the timeline of your book and see if everything that happens is in the right order.

I don't know about you, but I write my manuscripts on and off and usually over months (if not years), so it's easy to miss that the characters have lived through two Tuesdays in a row, or that you've forgotten to mention that it's been five months between the opening chapter and the end of the book.

It's also likely that edits might remove a reference to an event or the event altogether, but your characters may be dealing with the consequences in chapter sixteen.

Check...

- Every event that happens in your book—big and small.

- Ensure those events are happening in the order they're supposed to.

- Look out for day, month, season, or year mentions.

If your characters meet on a Monday, but the next scene is a Saturday, the reader might wonder what happened to the rest of the week. Get your timeline, events, days, months, seasons, years in order so your story is as plausible as possible.

The Plot Twists

While a plot twist doesn't happen every chapter, the foreshadowing, and the aftermath of each plot twist needs to be present in the lead-up chapters and the ones that follow the twist.

As you give your chapters a read for the millionth time...

- Highlight any foreshadowing and plot twist consequence.
- Confirm they're enough/work.
- Make sure they're in the right place for the story.

The Mix

As you're concentrating on each chapter, monitor...

- Description.
- Dialogue.
- Action.
- Setting.

Highlight (in different colors) each sentence that contains those things so you can see if the chapter contains enough of a mix.

This check may make you realize the chapter is super dialogue-heavy and could use a little more action to break it up. Or you may notice you've forgotten to add in the room setting so the reader can picture where your characters are as they make life-changing decisions during the climax of the book.

It's the little details of descriptions and settings, and the combination of dialogue and action that moves your story along, so getting the mix right is important.

Related Checklists

The Plot Twist Checklist
The Under Writing Checklist
The Over Writing Checklist
The Book Openings Checklist
The Chapter Endings Checklist
The Scene Sequel Checklist

The Chapter Checklist

☐ Choose Your Option and Weapons
Work from physical printouts or your screen using digital highlighters and note-taking features in your preferred writing program.

- Print out your manuscript.
- Staple each chapter together.
- Get/use highlighters for highlighting.
- Get/use Post-its for notes.
- Get/use a red/colored pen for corrections.

☐ The Length
- Check if any chapter lengths need to be adjusted.
- Too long? Cut it down or split it up.
- Too short? Brainstorm if more detailed descriptions or an extra scene, etc. will help.

☐ The Openings and Endings
- Check the first sentence/paragraph of every chapter one after the other to confirm you haven't opened any too similarly.
- Check the ending of each chapter to ensure there's a hook, cliffhanger, or closure.

☐ The Balance
- Read each scene in your chapter.
- Work out if it's a scene or a sequel.
- Ensure there's a balance of both.
- Highlight any unanswered questions to confirm you have some.
- Highlight the answers to those questions to also ensure you have them.

If you don't have a good balance of scenes, sequels, and unanswered questions, or there are questions that still need answers, note them down to fix.

 The Chapter Checklist

◯ The Timeline
- Check every event in your book—big and small.
- Ensure those events are happening in the order they're supposed to.
- Look out for day, month, season, or year mentions to confirm they're correct.

◯ The Plot Twists
- Highlight any foreshadowing and plot twist consequences.
- Confirm they're enough/work.
- Make sure they're in the right place for the story.

◯ The Mix
As you're concentrating on each chapter, highlight (in a different color) each sentence that contains...

- Description.
- Dialogue.
- Action.
- Setting.

This is to see if the chapter contains a mix of all and that they're in the right balance for the story.

The Little Details Checklist

THERE'S SO MUCH TO keep on top of when writing a book that it's easy to forget the little details, like what your characters are wearing or what movie they saw on the first date with their love interest.

While you might think such things aren't super special to know, or that you wouldn't let them slip past you, it's the little details that fill in your book world. Keeping track of them is important, especially when you're on draft eleventy and have read the story so many times everything's blurred together.

Luckily, there is a way you can make sure you don't leave out the little-yet-important details, and it's with the tips listed here.

To get the full benefit of this checklist, your manuscript should be at the final draft or close to it.

Have it in front of you, either printed out or on screen, and get out a notebook (not the fancy one, of course!), a scrap of paper, or your fave note-taking app or program and write these checklist headings on their own page...

- Unanswered questions.
- Who knows what.
- Character fashion.
- Callbacks.
- Loose threads.
- Reader reminders.

- Secrets.

As you read through your manuscript from start to finish (yes, *yet* again), keep an eye out for these elements during each scene, and under the right heading, jot down the details.

Unanswered Questions

These are those page-turning treasures of info, off-handed comments, seeds of doubt, and dialogue bombshells that spark a question for the reader—one that they'll *want* an answer to.

- Scour your scenes for unanswered questions.
- Look for the answers
- Write them both down.

By the last page of your manuscript, each question should have been answered with satisfaction, or enough info that an answer will be forthcoming in a future book if you're writing a sequel or a series.

If you haven't answered the question, or this check has brought to light that your unanswered question and its answer are weak, note it down so you can fix it.

Who Knows What

- Under this heading/page, you'll keep straight who knows what.

Let's say, for example, that your main character tells his girlfriend he was totally at his best friend's house studying when he was really at *her* best friend's house "studying."

Keeping straight that the main character's girlfriend and his best friend *don't* know about the cheating, but that the main character and the girlfriend's best friend *do*, is the type of info *you'll* need to know to either hide or reveal the affair.

Your story might not have such a scandalous twist, but if it has any type of info that only certain characters know and others don't, pop it down.

Having an easy reference to the ins and outs of who knows what will ensure any truth bomb reveals or this-character-doesn't-know-this-info-yet scenarios don't cause confusion.

Character Fashion

Unless the fashion of your characters is integral to the plot of your book, it's easy to make up what someone is wearing and then forget what you wrote for the next three drafts. But what characters wear adds realness, so it's a little detail that can make a big impact.

- Note down every outfit a character wears, including type and color.

They might change outfits many times, only once, not at all, or you may not have noticed that side character 2 and 3 wear the same color dress. Noting these details down means you can fix errors in your next edit, and that you'll also have a reference for what a character wore without having to comb through thirty chapters.

Callbacks

One fun writer's trick to add to your novel is calling back to something already mentioned.

Whether it's the love interest's favorite song, a parent reminding the main character of a childhood toy, or an inside joke mentioned at the start of the book that can then break the tension in a closing chapter, you can amp up the nostalgia for both your readers and the characters with a well-placed callback.

To do this, use the *Callbacks* checklist heading to write…

- Tidbits.
- Character quirks.
- Character memories you want to reference.
- Anything that will be worth referencing later.

That way, when you need a final emotional heartstring pulled, a shared joke between friends brought back up, or a line of dialogue repeated to drive home a point, you'll have a handy list of callbacks to draw upon.

Loose Threads

This checklist item is for anything you come across in your read through that needs...

- To be addressed by the end of the story.
- Removed for clarity.

You may have cut out the package arrival of a certain item during the great cull of draft 5 and are now scrambling to explain why the villain has what they need to foil the main character. Or you may have mentioned an annoying sibling in a throwaway line during draft 2, and failed to notice they're never featured again.

Get your running list of loose threads going so that any left dangling can be cut, sewn into place, or left appropriately hanging.

Reader Reminders

Sometimes in your story you'll need the readers to remember something specific.

It could be that your main character is allergic to peanuts right before he's about to be fed peanut-laced food, or that the murder victim wrote the password to his laptop on the back of a takeout menu.

It's information that the reader *needs to know*, but is often something you'll foreshadow early, or only once, so a reminder is usually needed closer to the twist or reveal so you can nail your payoff.

Under this heading...

- Note down any reminders that readers will need.
- Check that they're either in place or plan where they need to be placed within your plot to pull them off.

Secrets

If your book is full of secrets, you'll most definitely need a simple way to keep track of them—cue the final checklist item—*secrets*.

Under this heading, put down...

- What the secret is.
- When it's hinted at.
- When it's revealed.
- Who knows what.
- When a character knows the secret.

Trying to keep track of secrets can be a confusing business, and if the secret is a game-changing revelation, you don't want to mess it up.

Like everything listed here, getting secrets right will help make your book the best it can be, so use this checklist to perfect the little details, and see it naturally enhance your big book moments, too.

Related Checklists

The Foreshadowing Checklist
The Distinct Characters Checklist

The Little Details Checklist

○ **Gather Your Draft**

To get the full benefit of this checklist, your manuscript should be at the final draft or close to it.

- Print it out or look at it on a screen.
- Use a (non-fancy) notebook or your favorite note-taking app.
- Write the following checklist headings on their own page.
- Make notes in each appropriate section for things to know/fix.

○ **Unanswered Questions**

- Scour your scenes for unanswered questions.
- Look for the answers
- Write them both down.
- Each question should be answered or left with enough info if it'll be addressed in a different book.

○ **Who Knows What**

If there's any type of info that only certain characters know and others don't, pop it down.

○ **Character Fashion**

Note every outfit a character wears, including type and color.

The Little Details Checklist

○ **Callbacks**
- Write down tidbits.
- Character quirks.
- Character memories you want to reference.
- Anything that will be worth referencing later.

○ **Loose Threads**
- Anything that needs to be addressed by the end of the story.
- Things that can be removed for clarity.
- A running list of loose threads so any left dangling can be cut, sewn into place, or left appropriately hanging.

○ **Reader Reminders**
- Note down any reminders that readers will need to pull off plot twists or reveals.
- Check that they're either in place or plan where they need to be placed within your plot to pull them off.

○ **Secrets**
- What the secret is.
- When it's hinted at.
- When it's revealed.
- Who knows what.
- When a character knows the secret.

The Repeats Checklist

IF YOU'VE EVER EDITED a manuscript, you'll know it takes many drafts and rewriting to shape it into a readable book. Amongst those drafts should be a pass that includes finding a word that is repeated so much that you could turn it into a drinking game.

I call these instances *The Repeats*; a list of words that I know my *writing-self* likes to cram into sentences, but my *editor-self* knows shouldn't be there.

My personal *Repeats* list includes...

- Though.
- Realize/Realise/Realized/Realise.
- Took.
- Stood.
- Surprise/Surprised.
- Doubt.

These are the words that flow during a first draft and then survive the rest of the drafts because they're so ingrained in my writing voice that I don't even notice them.

When looking at these words amongst others, it's easy to think that they've been used sparingly, but with a *Repeats Checklist* run during the revision process, it's plain to see that isn't the case at all.

Taking Care of the Repeats

Accumulate a List

If you'd like to take care of your repeats, accumulate a list by noting...

- Words you've used a lot.

- Phrases you repeat (such as that old chestnut of every character *holding a breath*).

Find Your Repeats

Catching *The Repeats* is as simple as using the *find/search* tool (sometimes listed as *Find and Replace*, depending on your program).

Find

- Use your writing program to *find/search* the word/phrase.

- Check each chapter at a time, going to the highlighted word/phrase.

- Read the sentence it's in and...

Replace Your Repeats

Once you've found the repetitive word/phrase...

- Replace it with another word/phrase that suits.

- Or rewrite the sentence to eliminate it.

It's that easy—and that hard.

Tips for the Repeats

Sometimes you'll find that not only have you used a word repeatedly throughout the whole manuscript, but *multiple times* in a chapter, scene, and even in the same sentence.

- Decide on your allowed limit of a word/phrase per scene, chapter, or entire book, and stick to it.

This goes double for a word that readers don't automatically glaze over. If it's an unusual word like *indubitably*, it'll stick out like a sore thumb. Coming across such a word once usually gains attention, seeing it five or six times throughout the rest of the book just highlights it in the reader's mind, causing the word to lose its impact.

- A great word used once brings home the point. The same great word repeated every other chapter doesn't.

Whilst you might wonder how you replace common words, *The Repeats* are *not* words such as *The*, *Said*, *He*, *She*, or *That*.

- They are words that are used repeatedly in the same way.

If you look back at my personal list, you'll see *Realize/Realized*. They're listed because of the following sentences that were once in the *same chapter* of an early draft in my Blackbirch series:

— When he **realized** he was too far back to come to a conclusion, he slid out of the bed.
— He **realized** that the T-shirt was also white.
— They were in a waiting room, he **realized**.
— It took him a few seconds to **realize** she was referring to his earlier question.

Gets repetitive, doesn't it? Changing all but one of these *Repeats* in subsequent drafts made for a better read.

Now, for our final tip...

- Make your replacements new and natural.

Don't just turn to the thesaurus and pick out the fanciest word because it still says what you want but reads nothing like the word you're replacing.

It's like on the TV show *Friends* when Joey writes a letter of recommendation to an adoption agency on behalf of Monica and Chandler. He uses a thesaurus to turn "They are warm, nice, people with big hearts" into "They are humid prepossessing Homo sapiens with full-sized aortic pumps."

Don't be a Joey. Replace your repeats responsibly with new and natural options and reap the benefits.

Related Checklists

The Weak Words Checklist

The Repeats Checklist

◯ Accumulate a List
Create a personal list of words and phrases that your writing-self likes to cram into sentences, but your editor-self knows shouldn't be there.

Examples:
- Though.
- Realize/Realise/Realized/Realised.
- Took.
- Stood.
- Surprise/Surprised.
- Doubt.

◯ Find Your Repeats
Use the *find/search* tool of your writing program.

- Enter a word from your repeats list and hit *find/search* so every instance is highlighted.
- Enter a phrase from your repeats list and hit *find/search* so every instance is highlighted.
- Check each chapter, one at a time.
- Read the sentence the repeated word/phrase is in and...

◯ Replace Your Repeats
Once you've found the repetitive word/phrase, replace it with another word/phrase that suits or rewrite the sentence to eliminate it.

◯ Tips for the Repeats
- Set a limit of a word/phrase per scene, chapter, or book, and stick to it.
- A great word used once brings home the point. The same great word repeated every other chapter doesn't.
- Don't use a thesaurus to pick the fanciest version of a repeat so it still says what you want but reads differently. Replace the repeated word with something new/different or delete.

Afterword

Well, you've made it to the very end and are no doubt sick of the word *checklist*. That's to be expected.

Another expectation is that you learned something new, and now have helpful resources to achieve your writing and editing goals. If you do, my job here is done, and I wish you all the best shaping your manuscript into the greatest book *you* can make!

If you'd like more items to tick off, my website has a companion ebook, which you can download for *free* at this link: https://kmallan.com/authoring-checklists.

I hope you enjoy it just as much as you have this book.

Authoring Checklists
Tips and Tricks for Being a Modern Writer

Becoming an author is more than typing words onto a page. It's the endless battle against procrastination, keeping motivated through rejection, and taking your 80,000 words of hard work and distilling it into a one-page synopsis!

Enter the *Authoring Checklists*. They cover everything writing that *isn't* writing, and what's required of authors in a modern world, such as writing habits, style sheets, series bibles, stopping self-sabotaging, and dealing with self-doubt. There are even checklists to help you write a query letter, blurb, and put together an ARC!

Along with advice for sorting feedback, dealing with rejection, branding your social media and other tips, this book will help you up your Authoring game, regardless of whether you've been in the trenches for years or are just starting out.

Thank You!

Thank you for reading **Writing and Editing Checklists: Everything You Need to Take Your Book From First Draft to Publication**.

If this book has helped your creative endeavors, please consider leaving a review wherever you can (even just a sentence or a star rating will do), and recommend the book to a friend, the writing community, or on your socials.

Reviews get the word out about independently published books and are very much needed and appreciated.

Acknowledgements

First off, a huge thankyou and shout-out to the blogging community that embraced this content and gave me the encouragement to turn it into a book.

Eternal thanks to my alpha reader and friend, Meelie (M.L. Davis). Your excitement for this book was beyond inspiring and no-one's a better *Typo Hunter* than you. I'm so grateful we found each other through the blogging community and look forward to championing each other's work in the years to come.

My betas and #FrontRowNerds, Belinda Grant, and K.D. Kells. Your help shaping the content was invaluable and deserves a thousand thanks with an extra special thanks to Belinda for the excellent book blurbs. We've all known each other for years now and I'm a richer writer because of your friendship, support, library writing sessions, and our annual writing retreats.

Thank you to the incredible Katya de Becerra for the wonderful front cover endorsement and for both reading and recommending my blog to others. It is very much appreciated.

This wouldn't be a complete acknowledgment section without a nod to the #6amAusWriters whose virtual company and motivation makes the early morning writing sessions worth getting out of bed for.

A big thank you to Derek for once again taking my vague ideas and graphic mockups and turning them into awesome book covers.

Last, but not least, thank you to my family for their ongoing support, and my writing buddies, Dash, and Luna, who know how to steal my chair during all the important moments.

About the Author

K.M. Allan is an identical twin, but not the evil one. She started her career penning beauty articles for a hairstyling website and now powers herself with chocolate and green tea while she writes novels and blogs about writing.

Her debut series, *Blackbirch*—a 4-book modern urban fantasy about dark secrets and magical abilities is a hit with readers, receiving multiple 4 and 5-star reviews, and each appearing in the top 5 on *Amazon's Hot New Release* bestseller list upon release.

When not writing, she likes to read, binge-watch too much TV, spend time with family, and take more photos than she will ever humanly need.

Visit her website, www.kmallan.com, to discover the mysteries of the universe. Or at the very least, some good writing tips.

Welcome to Blackbirch. It's a place no one forgets. Except for Josh Taylor.

To restore his memories and find the true cause of his parents' death, Josh must learn what's real, what's a nightmare, and what secrets his home town of Blackbirch has buried in its woods.

Lost memories, premonitions, magical abilities, friendships, frenemies, first love, and dark secrets abound in this Young Adult series that's been hailed as...

"...action-packed & loaded with plot twists & turns...".

Review quote source: Goodreads.
Available now in paperback and ebook - kmallan.com/blackbirch

www.ingramcontent.com/pod-product-compliance
Lightning Source LLC
Chambersburg PA
CBHW022031290426
44109CB00014B/821